Birds
Everywhere

BIRDS

EVERYWHERE

BY JEAN DORST

Curator of Birds and Mammals at the Museum of Natural History, Paris

PICTURES BY PIERRE PROBST

WHITMAN PUBLISHING COMPANY

RACINE, WISCONSIN

Contents

Introduction

Today, throughout the world, far-seeing men are making a plea to save what is left of the natural beauties and awe-inspiring wonders that have been given Man—a plea to look around and rediscover the sea, the forest, the swampland, the mountains, the sky, and all the creatures that make up this wonderful world. There is much to be seen, much to marvel at, and not the least is the brilliant world of birds. Birds have suffered as man has drained marshland, cut down sheltering brush, and claimed the earth and sky for his own. But, in spite of their struggle, today as always birds play an important part in the world in which we live.

Far back in history, birds were observed and their habits noted. The Bible contains many references to birds and their ways. Early Man drew pictures of birds on cave walls; American Indians and early Egyptians wove birdlike forms into their religious thinking. The Eagle became the symbol of strength and power; the Dove of gentleness and peace.

Because of their color, song, and movement, birds are more readily observed than any other form of wildlife. The quick, nervous movement of a House Sparrow along a city street or in a cluttered alley attracts the city dweller. The clear whistle of the Meadowlark, the dash of color as a Cardinal flies across the road, the eerie call of a Screech Owl near a camping site, the strange, splattering run of a Coot as it takes off from a lake arouse the attention of the most casual observer.

Birds are found the world over and it is not strange that they have become a part of the life of all people. No matter where you are, birds are your neighbors. They are found in polar regions, in tropical forests,

in swamps, woodlands, along the seashores, in arid regions. Some feed on insects, some on seeds and fruits, small animals and snakes. Because of their specialized feeding, a certain kind of bird may be found in a region where its particular food is abundant, and the destruction of this food supply may endanger the very existence of this species. Birds are creatures of habit; their lives are ruled by instinct. They have no ability to think as Man does although amateur bird watchers sometimes erroneously interpret bird actions by human standards. So, because a bird's whole life is pre-determined, it is often difficult, if not impossible, for it to change its habits.

Bird watching is not confined to any particular group of people. A boy of ten or twelve, a foundry worker, a college professor, an executive, and a housewife may all equally enjoy the experience of searching for birds and studying their habits. Patience, time, and a healthy curiosity are all that is required; a good bird book and a pair of binoculars are useful aids. Contrary to common thought, it is not necessary to travel far to watch birds, and it is often more interesting to study the actions of one bird than to seek out a record number. If the watcher is quiet and slow in his movements, the bird will often come within his range of vision.

To watch birds, to observe their beauty, their way of life, their similarities and differences, is an absorbing and often exciting hobby. The actions of birds in yards, parks, and nearby countryside can easily be observed, but few people are fortunate enough to travel the world over to become acquainted with the bird life in distant places. It is for these people—child, youth, and adult—that this book is prepared.

THE EDITORS

Where Do Birds Live?

FAMILIAR birds crowd around our doors—Robins, Sparrows, Purple Martins, Chickadees, Warblers, Bluebirds, and Grackles, to name only a few. And yet if we mentioned all these birds to a schoolboy from Equatorial Africa, to a little Indian from the forests of the Amazon, or to a young Javanese, they would sound strange, for to these children they would all be exotic birds.

In return, the African Negro would tell us of thousands of Waxbills which he sees in the fields, of Parrots with gray plumage trimmed with red, of Guinea Fowl with dark feathers finely speckled with white, and of quantities of Ducks and long-legged Herons and Storks. The Latin American Indian would talk of Macaws with long balancing tails, of Quetzals in their royal finery, of the Scarlet Ibis which stand out on the sandbanks like scarlet spots, of brilliantly colored Manakins and of Tinamous and their strange cries. A Javanese would not find it hard to tell us the names of the birds he sees every day outside his hut or in the paddy fields, all of them unknown to us, except for those which we may have seen at the zoo.

Because of their successful invasion of the air, birds became distributed all over the globe, from polar regions to the equator. There are roughly 8,600 species of birds which are divided into 25,000 recognizable geographical varieties, having different structural and functional modifications.

Birds are not distributed evenly all over the world. Some of the more easily adaptable ones, like the English Sparrow, can be found in almost any climate. Others, like the shore birds, such as Sandpipers and Plovers, which enliven our beaches in spring and in autumn, cover the entire globe in the course of their annual migrations. Still others seem to be found everywhere: in every port of the world we think we see the same Gulls and sea birds, but an expert would be able to distinguish different species from among those birds which at first seem identical.

12

Skua
Ptarmigan
Auk
Swan
Goose
Wader
Warbler
Robin
Tit
Redstart
Woodpecker
Raven
Gull
Flamingo
Pheasant
Bustard
Ostrich
Weaverbird
Shoebill
Guinea-Fowl
Ibis
Woodpecker
Hornbill
Crane
Weaverbird
Cassowary
Toucan
Wood Ibis
Parrot
Cockatoo
Parrot
Crowned Pigeon
arakeet
Woodpecker
Bird of Paradise
Marabou
Lyrebird
Kiwi
Laughing Jackass
Albatross

Many birds are characteristic of a particular part of the world. Often they are found in very well-defined areas. Birds of Paradise are found in New Guinea, Lyrebirds in Australia, and the Toucans only in South America.

There are many more kinds of birds in the tropics than in cold climates. Hot countries are rich in food for birds, in flowers, fruits, and insects all the year round. Birds flourish there and many have come to be associated in our minds with the favored regions in which they live. Who, for instance, can imagine seeing a Parrot, or a Hornbill with its enormous beak, or a Curassow anywhere but amid tropical vegetation?

On the other hand, some birds have adapted themselves to cold countries, and even to polar regions. Geese and Swans nest in the far north where innumerable sea birds, such as Auks, Guillemots, and Petrels also live. Antarctica is the kingdom of the Penguins, but they also may be found on the Galapagos Islands at the equator.

Although most birds live on land, some have chosen the oceans for their homes. The Albatross and the Petrel live on the high seas all the year round and come ashore only to lay eggs and bring up their young. The fact that they may be found even in the middle of the ocean shows that every inch of the globe is inhabitable by birds.

POWER FLIGHT

SOARING FLIGHT

DIVING

SWIMMING

What Is a Bird?

1. Scapular
2. Wing Covert
3. Secondary Remiges
4. Primary Remiges
5. Tail Feathers

PHEASANT FEATHERS

Down   Contour Feather   Wing Feather

A BIRD is a feathered animal whose bone structure is adapted for flying. Birds are also physiologically constructed for flying. They are warm-blooded, have a high metabolic rate, and have a large, four-chambered heart which separates oxygenated blood from blood carrying body waste.

These small animals have a framework of bone, light but strong. Every bone is hollow to lessen its weight. Aluminum alloy tubes are used in building aircraft following this same principle. The forelimbs, which become wings in birds, are attached to the skeleton. This "airfoil," which is like the wing on an aircraft, can also be moved in a complex manner which causes the bird to travel through air. The cross section of a bird's flight feather is convex above and concave beneath. When such a wing section or feather is drawn through the air, the airstream passes more rapidly over the top than underneath because the distance across the top is greater. A suction, or "lift," is created on the upper surface and this action is the entire basis of flight. One of the first men to discover the principle of flight was the great Italian painter Leonardo da Vinci. He made himself a pioneer of aviation by studying in detail the wings and the flight of birds.

BILLS AND FEET

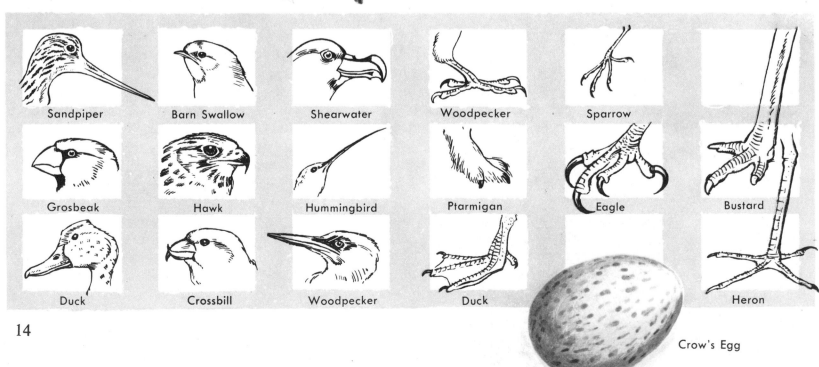

Sandpiper   Barn Swallow   Shearwater   Woodpecker   Sparrow

Grosbeak   Hawk   Hummingbird   Ptarmigan   Eagle   Bustard

Duck   Crossbill   Woodpecker   Duck   Heron

Crow's Egg

14

OUR FEATHERED FRIENDS

ORNITHOLOGY, the science of birds, has thousands of followers throughout the world. As the late Frank Chapman, a great American ornithologist, used to remark, "Everyone is born with a bird in his heart." Perhaps this explains the widespread existence of bird clubs and societies throughout the world and particularly in the United States. Kings and emperors have been first-class bird watchers, and some have even written books on their favorite pastime. Generals became interested in the birds they saw on campaigns in distant lands.

The first "American" ornithologist was Christopher Columbus, who tells of his meetings with many birds of the New World. But it was not until the time of J. J. Audubon, who may be called the father of American ornithology, that the study of birds was considered with respect in this country. The influence of Audubon is still very much felt.

Doubtless, ornithology has a greater following here than in any country of the world. This is explained by the richness and variety of our birds which range from Hummingbirds originating in the tropics to Snow Geese whose homes are the icy wastes of the far north. The great variety of species has enabled individual states to choose their specific birds for emblems. For example, the state bird of California is the California Quail, of Maine the Chickadee, of Maryland the Baltimore Oriole, New York the Bluebird, Virginia the Cardinal, and Pennsylvania the Ruffed Grouse.

Ornithologists estimate there are about 8,600 different species of birds living in the world. More than 650 can be found in North America. This gives a tremendous scope to bird lovers. Competitions are held every year, and on the big day bird watchers get up early, well before sunrise, and observe as many birds as possible before midnight. The participants organize their day in detail and travel from one place to another at the times calculated to give them the best opportunity of seeing the largest possible number of species. The present record of 173 species perfectly recognized and identified by a single person in a single day is a feat that will be difficult to surpass in the United States.

Birds are around us everywhere. It is estimated that there are about six billion land birds in the United States. Some regions of the country are densely populated with birds and others have very few, but on the average there are three birds to every acre.

Some kinds of birds are, of course, far more numerous than others. Whereas the Red-Eyed Vireo is without question the commonest of all birds in the eastern states, where its numbers run into millions, other kinds are represented now by less than one hundred individuals. There are only about eighty California Condors. Whooping Cranes are rarer still, and the Ivory-Billed Woodpecker, once a native of the southeast United States, is close to extinction.

Myrtle Warbler

Yellow-Throated Vireo

Robin

European Starling

Common Grackle

City Birds

NOTHING seems less favorable to bird life than a great modern city with its skyscrapers, its gigantic bridges, and its busy, paved streets. Yet large numbers of birds have managed to adapt themselves to the new conditions of city living. City planners have taken care to reserve parks, often vast ones, which are a paradise for birds and ornithologists. The bird watcher may see four hundred species in the region of New York City, including the migratory birds which pass through only in spring and autumn. Two hundred and thirty kinds of birds are known to have been seen in Central Park located in the heart of New York.

Of course you would have to be very patient to see such a record number, but you do not have to search long for Robins, which hop by the hundreds on the grass, looking for worms and insects which are the food of these pretty birds with red breasts. The popular Flicker is there, too, and you are not likely to overlook him because of his noisy cry. There are also countless Common Grackles, their black feathers shining with metallic reflections. These city dwellers see many of their country cousins arrive with the coming of autumn. Starlings are among the most numerous. They come in such vast flocks that they can become intolerable. Many methods have been tried to drive the Starlings away, but most of them have failed.

The trees of the avenues and the park bushes are the chosen domains of thousands of Warblers and Flycatchers, all looking for insects. Every patch of greenery they alight upon is enlivened by their fluttering and their singing and in the case of many of them by their bright coloring. A summer resident seeming to give not a thought to traffic and the crowds is the Baltimore Oriole. Its nest, when built, resembles a long purse. One of the most beautiful songsters of the great American cities is the Red-Eyed Vireo.

Just a few flowers attract the Ruby-Throated Hummingbird, the only representative of this family in the eastern United States. Hummingbirds, however, are much more varied in the west where several kinds may be found, some of them no bigger than a large insect. Ruby-Throated Hummingbirds migrate every year as far as Central America.

Swift

Rock Dove

European Blackbird

English Sparrows

Even birds of prey have sometimes chosen to live in the heart of cities. Duck Hawks, swift-flying Falcons which originally lived on cliffs, have been known to find the roofs of large buildings and the narrow ledges of skyscrapers convenient places to build their nests.

A bird which flourishes in city environments is the English Sparrow, introduced to Brooklyn from Europe in about 1850. It has since multiplied a millionfold. Called the House Sparrow in its native land, a name by which it is also known here, this bird is less of a pest in the city than in the countryside where it feeds on fruit buds and makes war on small native birds, particularly the Swallows. Swallows and House Martins, which belong to the same family, are insect eaters and thus beneficial to the farmer. Sparrows prevent their nesting on the eaves of farm buildings, so instead of the graceful, almost silent flight of Swallows, farmers are confronted with the noisy, continuous chirping of the English Sparrow.

The domestic Pigeon, a bird which came over with the first settlers, is also a common sight in the cities. There are believed to be more than 300,000 in the New York City area alone. Their nests are perched on the narrow ledges of buildings which take the place of the rocks where their ancestors, the wild Pigeons, once made their homes.

The Starling, however, is the bird which has benefited most from the congregation of men in urban communities. Six Starlings were imported from Europe in 1890 and were released in Central Park, New York City. They have since flourished to such an extent that now they number about 140,000 in the city of New York alone, and have spread throughout the United States, southern Canada, and northeastern Mexico. When autumn comes, the Starlings gather in roosts, sometimes as many as 100,000 at a time, and huddle together as if to keep each other warm on cornices of buildings, girders of bridges, and even in such respected places as the Capitol in Washington. This bird is really a foreigner among American birds, and yet it is one of the most common birds in the United States at the present time.

17

Garden Birds

Great Tit

Oriole

Chaffinch

Bullfinch

Wren

Redstart

KINGS and princes used to go to great expense to keep menageries where they reared costly tropical birds. Peacocks brightened royal parks with their brilliant plumage. Today, for those of us who know when and how to look, menageries rivaling those of the great men of the world can be found in and near our own gardens.

To take advantage of the possibilities our surroundings afford, we should get up at dawn with the birds and enjoy the concert which greets the rising sun. At our door we may find a flock of Chickadees searching the branches of a tree for insects, caterpillars, or delicious young shoots. A whistle may bring them quite close without their showing the slightest fear.

A House Wren may have set up its general headquarters in an old wall with accommodating holes in it. These mischievous, noisy birds are so well adapted to civilization that they happily build their nests in a nesting box left at their disposal. They have been known to nest in old hats left in garden sheds and even in a pocket of a pair of trousers hung up to dry on a line.

Warblers of all kinds babble in the trees, particularly the Yellow Warblers, dressed from head to tail in golden yellow clothes. Yellow-Throated Vireos are recognized by their hoarse, scolding cries. Other familiar garden birds are the Goldfinches. Their magnificent yellow plumage, trimmed with black on the head, wings, and tail, makes them easily recognizable. They are even found in built-up areas where they often settle.

The most distinguished of our American birds is the Cardinal. The male is a magnificent red, while his more reserved mate is of a much browner color. When on the move, this bird looks like a flame darting through the trees. Its beauty fully justifies the poems and books which have been dedicated to it. Cage-bird lovers in other parts of the world go to great pains to rear this bird in captivity, but we in the United States are able to see it in its natural state.

At the onset of spring, the Bluebirds return to our orchards. These birds, which often build in holes in old fruit trees, can easily be recognized by their splendid azure-blue backs contrasting beautifully with their cinnamon-red breasts. If we have had the forethought to put nesting boxes around the house, we will be pleased to see Bluebirds taking to them. What pleasure one can get from these beautifully colored birds and their sweet voices! What is more, they are tireless insect hunters and help to keep our gardens free of prolific pests.

One can often see Orioles in the orchards. In addition to the Baltimore Oriole, which builds its nest like a safe, hanging pocket in a tree, we can see Red-Winged Blackbirds which nest in marshes and beside ponds but come to search for insects among the trees. The male bird can be easily recognized by his red and buff epaulets contrasting with his otherwise black feathers.

Scarlet Tanager

Phoebe

Blackcap

Bluebird

Goldfinch

Yellow-Throated Vireo

Kingbird

European Goldfinch

Meadow Lark

Red-Winged Blackbird

Of course there is every chance that we will see Grackles on the lawn. No insect escapes their notice, be it a beetle, a grasshopper, or a weevil.

A proud and determined-looking bird stations itself on some conspicuous perch, perhaps a fence post or a bare branch protruding from the foliage of a tree. It is clearly a Kingbird, its head marked with a vivid orange splash almost hidden by dull gray feathers. As soon as an insect passes by, the Kingbird is after it like a flash. Then, after performing some lively acrobatics, it returns to its observation post. The Kingbird shows remarkable courage and, without hesitation, attacks such large birds as Hawks and Crows which it seems especially to hate.

Many other birds may come to our gardens, so we have no excuse for not becoming bird watchers. It is no use arguing that we have neither the time nor the means to go to distant places. In our own gardens and parks there are as many secrets to be uncovered as we could wish for to fill a lifetime!

Forest Birds

Blue Jay

Red-Eyed Vireo

American Redstart

Ovenbird

Black-and-White Warbler

male keeps up a continuous song from morning till night, taking intermissions of no more than a few seconds. It untiringly repeats the same notes forming a monotonous phrase; from this it has received the nickname of "Preacher."

A call on two notes echoes from a corner of the forest. Growing louder, it sounds like "teacher, TEACHER...." We are hearing the Ovenbird which is frequently found in the forests of the eastern United States. Most passerines (the ornithologists' name for any songbird) move in little hops, but the Ovenbird walks with a measured gait, shaking its tail as it goes.

To attract the Redstart, one of the most lively forest birds, all that is needed is a tiny clearing. The bird is continually opening and closing its wings and tail and hopping to and fro. Its tail is marked with bright red spots in strong contrast with its otherwise black feathers.

The treetops and dense foliage are the realm of the large family of Warblers. One of the most easily recognizable is the Black-and-White Warbler, with its plumage striped in these colors. Like a Creeper or a Nuthatch, it spends most of its time surveying the tree trunks and branches, looking for insects hidden in crevices in the bark.

FORESTS are secretive places. Their dense foliage shelters activities which are hidden from prying eyes. Yet forests are full of birds which betray their presence by their singing.

The best woodland songbird is to be found among the Thrushes. The Veery, which inhabits moist woods all summer through, sings a whistled melody that becomes softer and softer. Its song is surpassed only by that of the Hermit Thrush, the unrivaled virtuoso of America.

The Red-Eyed Vireo may not be able to compete with the Thrushes for quality of voice, but it makes up for this lack by the quantity of its singing. The

Others, like the Black-Throated Green Warbler, prefer to hunt in dense foliage. The Chestnut-Sided Warbler, on the other hand, can be found only in open woods, where the trees have been thinned out and where the young saplings have not yet had time to grow. As soon as the underbrush grows again, this Warbler disappears to look for more suitable surroundings. The changes which have taken place in the eastern United States in the last hundred years have been ideal for this bird, for it has multiplied tremendously since then. It is now a common bird, although Audubon never saw more than one in his lifetime.

Jay

Buzzard

Tawny Owl

Tree-Creeper

Great Spotted
Woodpecker

European Robin

Kinglet

Nuthatch

Forests of coniferous, or cone-bearing, trees attract birds which are not found in any other environment. The most numerous Warblers of these forests are the Myrtle and Pine Warblers, living in the pine trees. We also find the Ruby-Crowned Kinglet and the Golden-Crowned Kinglet, tiny birds with bright scarlet or orange spots, like royal crowns, on their heads. Some of these little birds do not migrate but spend the entire winter in the pines without showing the slightest discomfort.

Other inhabitants of the forests are Woodpeckers. Some of these birds are very common in the eastern United States. Most Woodpeckers betray their presence by the drumming of their beaks on the trunks of trees. Not only does the Common Sapsucker, as

one of these Woodpeckers is called, fill the woods with the sound of its determined drumming, it also darts around its nesting area uttering loud cries. As its name suggests, it feeds on sap drawn from tree trunks by drilling a hole with its strong beak. The Hairy Woodpecker, like most other members of its large family, prefers insects to sap.

We cannot leave the woods without taking note of the Blue Jay, one of the most beautiful American birds and one of the easiest to spot, on account of its liveliness. In spite of its handsome appearance, the Blue Jay can be a dangerous enemy. It inspires terror in other birds for it has a keen liking for eggs and newly hatched fledglings. It often robs the nests of small birds, even though they are carefully hidden.

Field Birds

Partridge

Magpie

Pheasant

Bobwhite

I N autumn large flocks of Crows gather on the open fields of the eastern United States. These soberly dressed black birds are not very distinguished in appearance. Their dark plumage has only a slight metallic gloss to brighten it. Remarkable for their intelligence, rather than their beauty, they are among the most cunning of all flying creatures.

Their flocks are so finely organized that they even provide "police protection." While the flock is busy on the plains searching for food—insects, grain, young plants, and various kinds of refuse—sentinels are posted at strategic points. These lookouts warn their companions of the approach of any suspect, and if there is real danger, the whole flock takes off.

It is almost impossible for man, or dog, or any other large animal to come near a flock of Crows. The same precautions are taken in the evening when the flock rests in the trees. In one roost alone there may be thousands of birds.

Crows understand one another perfectly as they have a very rich vocabulary. Whereas *we* can hear only an unmusical cawing, Crows in fact make a great variety of different sounds, each one having a special meaning. The cawing of Crows has been recorded for experiments and carefully analyzed. These recordings are sometimes played back through amplifiers near a group of Crows. If the cry played back is the distress signal of a sentinel Crow which has sighted an enemy, the flock immediately flies off.

A similar intelligence is noticeable in their cousins, the Magpies. These birds are useful as they kill rodents and some insects harmful to agriculture, but they are also guilty of certain crimes. They are thieves and plunderers of nests. They sometimes eat other birds' eggs and defenseless fledglings, even prey on chicks in farmyards. Farmers try to check their numbers.

Plains, whether open country or fields broken up by hedges, are the paradise of game-bird hunters. One of the best-known game birds is the Bobwhite, or Quail as it is called in many parts of the United States. For most of the year these land birds live in coveys made up of several families. They search the fields for bits of grain and for insects which crawl on the ground. At nightfall each covey retires to a thicket where the birds form a close circle facing outward so that they can take flight at the slightest alarm.

In the spring can be heard the often repeated cry of the male, "Bobwhite.... Bobwhite," which explains how these charming birds got their name.

Hunters abroad have imported Bobwhites to some parts of Europe and now they can be seen in the fields of France. In return, our hunters have introduced game birds from the Old World. The greatest success has been the Ring-Necked Pheasant, which originally came from Transcaucasia, from where the Greeks and Romans imported them to Mediterranean Europe in ancient times.

George Washington asked General Lafayette to bring from France pairs of Pheasants for breeding in America. Since that time, this bird has settled happily in a large area covering twenty-four states from New England to Oregon. As many as sixteen million Pheasants have been shot in a single hunting season.

How curious are the ways of men, who go to great trouble and expense to import birds for the sake of killing them!

Rook

Hooded Crow

Carrion Crow

23

Mountain Birds

Chough

Alpine Chough

European Nutcracker

Clark's Nutcracker

Rock Thrush

Calliope Hummingbird

Citril Finch

Wall Creeper

SOME birds have made their homes in the mountains. Here they find the food and shelter they need. Mountains are a safe refuge for birds; they can escape from man more easily there than in the lowlands. Peace-loving birds move to higher ground and become true mountain dwellers.

This is the case of the Golden Eagle which is now found only in the western mountains. Golden Eagles construct their nests, enormous structures made of roughly intertwined branches, at the tops of tall trees. Here they raise their eaglets, each day carrying food to them which must often be brought from far away.

Bald Eagles have a larger distribution than Golden Eagles and inhabit all parts of North America. In the eighteenth century, after a spirited congressional debate on whether the Bald Eagle was a noble enough bird or not, the United States chose it for a national emblem. This Eagle is found throughout America, and since ancient times has been a symbol of courage, power, and majesty.

The food of Eagles is mainly fish. To a lesser extent, Eagles eat small mammals, amphibians, reptiles and small birds, but they seldom fly off with chickens as people suppose, nor with lambs or young children as some stories say. Sometimes they pursue a smaller bird and make it drop its catch which the eagle will snatch before the food has fallen to the ground.

The keen eyesight of the Eagle is proverbial. Like many birds of prey, it has enormous eyes. Its eyes weigh more than its brain and combine the faculties of the microscope and the telescope. Calculations have been made showing that the Eagle can see a hundred times better than man. Some birds of prey can pick out from more than a mile off a ball of feathers fluttering on the end of a piece of string. A man could not do this even if he used binoculars. Yet Eagles have to be able to do more than merely sight their prey. By bracing their wings they swoop down on their prey, quickly snare it, and carry it off to their eaglets.

Many smaller birds inhabit mountainous country. In the coniferous forests of the great western mountains live the Nutcrackers, cousins of the Crows, which have gray feathers and contrasting black wings. These birds are often seen around mountain hotels and chalets. During the summer they eat anything they find, but when winter comes, their princi-

pal food is the seeds of fir trees. They carefully collect fir cones and extract the seeds hidden between the scales, noisily displaying their satisfaction.

Birds are numerous on mountainous ground, and the height at which they can live is limited only by the vegetation available. One of our smallest Hummingbirds, the Calliope Hummingbird, has been seen at an altitude of ten thousand feet. It is more often found lower down on the edge of cone-bearing forests and mountain grasslands, where it helps itself to nectar from lupines, elephant heads, and other flowers which bloom when the snow has melted. The Red-Faced Warbler has been seen as high as eight thousand feet up on sunny slopes. Its favorite insect hunting ground is the tops of fir trees, where it meets many other birds, particularly the Cassin's Finch. The male Cassin's Finch has pink feathers with brownish markings.

Golden Eagle

25

Ocean Birds

Albatross

Shearwater

Stormy Petrel

Fulmar

best adapted of birds to marine life, Albatrosses go ashore only to build their nests, usually on islands in the South or North Pacific oceans.

Except for Petrels and certain of the Gulls, most other birds stay near shore where fish are abundant and the waves throw up refuse from passing ships. The Ring-Billed Gull, one of our most common Gulls, was so named because of the black ring which circles its beak. It has followed us inland and usually nests beside lakes.

The Herring Gull, its strong yellow beak trimmed with a bright red splash, is probably the most common bird along our shores. Thanks to its adaptability, intelligence, and vigor (it has been known to live as long as forty years in captivity) it is able to use almost everything thrown up by the sea, but it is also a plunderer, swallowing eggs and gobbling up baby birds when given the chance.

These habits can be seen more strongly developed in a group of birds which specialize in stealing. They are the Jaegers and Skuas, whose drab dress helps them to carry out their shady deeds. Not content with robbing nests, they look for a Tern which has just caught a fish, swoop down on the happy hunter, and pursue it mercilessly until it surrenders its catch. When the Tern gives up and lets go, the pirate quickly snares the prey before it drops into the sea.

During autumn, the deserted beaches are invaded by thousands of migrants. These little waders have left the Far North and are on their way to milder regions. They descend along the beaches in vast numbers. With hurried steps, Sandpipers and Plovers and other species of shore birds explore the beaches searching for food. When looking for a meal, some shore birds turn pebbles over with their beaks, and one of them thus earned its name of Turnstone.

Another beach invader, the Oyster Catcher, prefers mollusks which it can pick up and pry open with its flattened beak that looks somewhat like an oyster knife.

By feeding continually at the water's edge, birds of the seashore make sure that none of the riches of the sea are wasted when deposited on land. They are fortunate, for every tide replenishes their food supply.

THE sea, which covers three quarters of the world's surface, is full of animal life, from the smallest particle of plankton to enormous whales. It is not surprising, therefore, to find many sea birds taking advantage of this great food store.

The Albatross is the unrivaled king of the sea. One species has a wing span of twelve feet making it the largest of all flying birds. To take off, the Albatross runs on the surface of the water but once airborne, it can fly with the greatest of ease. It can also plane like a glider, without flapping its wings. The

Parasitic Jaeger

Herring Gull

Black-Headed Gull

Sandpiper

Curlew

Common Tern

Black Bellied Plover

Black-Headed Gull

Oyster Catcher

Turnstone

Marsh Birds

BECAUSE of its warm climate, Florida is a paradise for people and for birds who want to escape the winter. On both the Atlantic and the Gulf of Mexico shores, sun-soaked beaches stretch for hundreds of miles. Florida's hotels welcome tourists and businessmen worn out by the restless life of big cities, but they also welcome naturalists and ornithologists, for its aquatic jungles and luxuriant vegetation make Florida a wonderland of birds.

In the interior of this vast peninsula, land and water have melted into each other everywhere to form a landscape of extraordinary swamps. Reeds and palm trees blend with the famous bald cypresses, while in the water and along the banks plants climb and spread with amazing rapidity.

In the center of the peninsula is a lake covering several hundred square miles. It is Lake Okeechobee, which means "big water" in Seminole, the language of the local Indians.

The lake is the home of thousands of water birds. One of the strangest is the Anhinga or Water Turkey, cousin of the Cormorant. Its long, flexible neck supports an elongated head. These are the only parts of the bird visible when it is swimming. Thus it acquired its nickname of Snake Bird.

The most numerous birds in Florida are the Herons, of which there are several easily recognizable kinds: Great Blue Herons, American Egrets, Little Blue Herons, both Black-Crowned and Yellow-Crowned Night Herons, Snowy Egrets, Louisiana Herons, and Green Herons. Often several different species together build colonies in the low trees. The nests form a platform of branches where the young birds await food brought by the adult birds, who fly ceaselessly to and fro. An additional species of Heron has recently come to North America via Central America. It is the Cattle Egret, an immigrant from Europe.

The Wood Storks, formerly known as Wood Ibises, have chosen to live in the mangrove swamps of the Everglades National Park in southern Florida. Their white feathers contrast with the bare, blackish skin of their necks and heads, and the dark, bronze-green flight feathers. These large, sociable birds are found in the company of Glossy Ibises, clad in rich bay (reddish-brown) with shades of metallic purple and green, and White Ibises, entirely white except for black-tipped wings and bright carmine faces, beaks, and feet. Wood Storks are sometimes found with Roseate Spoonbills, whose beaks, flattened like spatulas, are well adapted for catching small fish, shellfish, and insects.

One of the rarest birds in the United States is the Everglade Kite, a day-flying bird of prey. Only about fifty individuals now remain in Florida. Originally the swampy Everglades abounded in large snails, and these were the Kite's food. This bird has a little hook bent back at the end of its beak. It uses this hook to extract a snail or a mollusk from its shell, which the bird holds firmly between its toes. The Limpkin, a distant cousin of the Rail, eats in the same manner, using its pincerlike beak to dig out the hidden snail from its shell.

Limpkin

Brown Pelican

Purple Gallinule

Many land birds have settled in Florida. There are Orioles with brilliant orange and golden-yellow feathers, as well as many very small birds such as Warblers, Vireos, and Hummingbirds.

We may also see Anis, relatives of the Cuckoo, which are common in South America but also firmly established in this State. These birds, with their black feathers, and beaks which are decorated with a sort of horny crest, could be confused with Grackles. However, they are very different. The sociable Anis build communal nests where several females lay their eggs in layers separated by leaves. The birds take turns sitting on the nest, and hatching is hastened by the heat given out by the fermenting leaves.

Anhinga

Black-Crowned
Night Heron

Wood Stork

White Ibis

Common Egret

Green Heron

Roseate Spoonbill

Great Blue Heron

Penduline Tit

Bee-Eater

Dartford Warbler

Spoonbill

Avocet

In the south of France there is a sunny stretch of country where fresh water and salt water blend with sand and mud. This is the Camargue, the triangle of land formed by the two branches of the Rhone River. The area has long been the home of herds of wild bulls and horses. Today rice is grown there, adding to the exotic character of this curious region.

The Camargue is a land of birds and above all is the haunt of Flamingos. Although we have an American species in captivity in Florida and in native colonies in the West Indies, this is the only flourishing community on the continent of Europe. A group of Flamingos at Hialeah race track in Florida furnishes about the best opportunity most of us have to see one alive. Their numbers are few in America because the Flamingo can only live in certain semi-tropical areas where is found a particular kind of small shellfish, and also because human raids on their colonies have seriously reduced their numbers. In

areas where it is not protected, the young Flamingo is hunted because it provides excellent eating.

These wading birds stand from four to six feet tall. Their heads are set atop long, slender necks. Balancing themselves on long legs, they probe the mud with angular beaks, equipped with a sort of horny filter, and, turning their heads upside down, they suck up tasty little salt-water shrimps. Flamingos gather in breeding "towns" located on the flats beside open salt-water lagoons. To build a nest, the Flamingo scoops up mud and sculpts a kind of pedestal on which a single egg is placed, protected from any sudden rising of the waters.

The baby Flamingo is restless by nature, the very opposite of its dignified elders. At a day old it will scramble out of the nest to trot around the colony, returning when the parents call it back home to be fed.

Marshes make the Camargue a paradise for wading

birds. Gray Herons, White Egrets, and Night Herons with their black caps adorn the stretches of water, as does the Avocet, a little black and white wading bird with a long beak like an upturned sickle. Strange plants grow around the ponds and salt marshes. Countless small passerines live among the delicate-leaved tamarisk, the salt-loving saltwort, and the sweet-smelling bushes. The Penduline Tit patiently collects vegetable rubbish to build its purse-like nest with walls as soft as felt. The Dartford Warblers spend most of their time in hiding, appearing only for a second perched in a comic posture on a branch or a twig.

The sides of enormous sand dunes are hollowed out by colonies of Bee-Eaters for their nests. These nests are tunnels more than three feet deep in which the young birds are sheltered from sun and rain. The brilliantly colored Bee-Eaters are African invaders which have settled in Europe.

Flamingo

Sacred Ibis

Crowned Crane

Spurwing Goose

Pelican

African Birds

THE continent of Africa was unexplored two thousand years ago and the fact of its being so gave rise to many legends among the Greeks and Romans. They believed it was a pillar supporting the heavens and that a race of mysterious, winged people lived there. If Aristotle could have visited Africa, he could have disproved many of these legends. He would have been amazed to discover a lake in Equatorial Africa.

Here he would have seen the Crowned Crane. This bird, its head adorned with a crown-like crest, is king of this richly colored world. Aristotle would also have seen Pelicans, comic-looking on land, and yet surprisingly majestic when they take flight and glide in the sun. Pelicans have excellent flying abilities, yet they do not seem to want to wander far from the shores on which they breed: around swampy districts, inland lakes and rivers, and the tidal waters of the ocean. To feed their young the parent Pelicans disgorge fish from their enormous membranous pouches by pressing their chests with their beaks.

In Africa nature has given full rein to her imagination. The Shoebill owes its name to a monstrous beak swollen into the form of a shoe. The Skimmer has a beak with which it skims the water in search of tiny animals which float on the surface of rivers and ponds. The Skimmer is a cousin of the Terns, whose beaks are flattened sideways like a pair of scissors. The African Skimmer lives only near fresh water and particularly beside rivers.

A common sight in Africa are the many palmipeds, or web-footed birds, which invade the sandbanks that are uncovered in the dry season. Among them are the Whistling Tree Ducks, whose presence may always be detected by their characteristic fluting whistle. Wading birds are far from rare. The most deserving of respect is the Sacred Ibis, with black and white plumage. The ancient Egyptians worshiped this bird as a god, and carefully preserved mummies have been found in the tombs of Upper Egypt.

The richly colored Saddle-Billed Stork may be seen together with its cousin the African Stork, but a bird which is notable less for its coloring than for its strange nesting habits is the Hammerhead. Small in size and brown in color, Hammerheads build enormous nests in huge trees. The nests, far bigger than their builders, are made of intertwined branches in the form of a sphere open at one side somewhat like a huge hornet's nest. A legend tells how these birds employ laborers for this work, making little birds carry materials which they have collected from an appointed place. The small birds are said later to come and live within the walls of the Hammerheads' nests, the latter being untroubled by these neighbors.

Another curious African bird is the Jacana, or Lily-Trotter, which is able to walk on water-lily leaves and other floating plants. The Lily-Trotter moves with great ease from one plant to another because of its enormous toes which enable its weight to be spread over a wide area.

We must also mention the millions of Herons and Egrets which bring color to the marshes. Some of these seem to have an agreement with the antelopes and often perch on their backs quite fearlessly. They quickly catch any insects uncovered by these animals and, in exchange, warn their hosts of approaching danger. This is an example of mutually advantageous cooperation between birds and mammals, and one which is very surprising considering the otherwise shy personality of the Heron. A solitary feeder, the Heron is often to be seen standing motionless in shallow water on the alert for food, usually fish which are caught by a sudden thrust of its long beak.

African Wood Ibis

ree Duck

Jacana

Saddle-Billed Stork

Shoebill

Hammerhead

Desert Birds

Red-Tailed Hawk

Le Conte's Thrasher

THE Colorado Grand Canyon presents a most magnificent panorama. But after visitors have taken in the spectacle, there is still much in the area to be seen. The vast desert is well worth a visit by the naturalist. The sparse vegetation has become adapted to the dry climate. Most of the plants, for instance the gigantic cacti, are covered with sharp thorns. Prickly pears form thick, thorny walls, and saguaros as tall as fifty feet and sometimes weighing more than twelve tons stand with their arms outstretched as if making strange signals. Elsewhere we may see Joshua trees protected by bunches of long, daggerlike leaves.

Although the desert appears hostile to animal life, it is inhabited by birds that have adapted themselves to its dry climate. One of the most interesting of these is the Roadrunner, a cousin of the Cuckoo, which thrives on the dry, bare ground, and which might at first be taken for a little Pheasant because of its size, its habits, and its buff and brown stripes. It shows little desire to fly and prefers to run along the ground. This explains its name, given to it by early settlers in the West. When surprised, the Roadrunner runs at full speed, as if to compete with the speed of its pursuer. It will suddenly swerve to one side and disappear into a thorny bush that looks quite impenetrable. The Roadrunner uses this side-stepping talent to chase lizards, which are its principal food. It will even attack snakes from whose bite it escapes with agility.

The saguaro cactus lives for about two hundred years. Long before it reaches an advanced age, its huge arms are pitted with many deep cavities, which are often occupied by squatters. The most important squatter is the Elf Owl, not more than five inches long, and thus one of the smallest Owls in the world. The Elf Owl finds a safe refuge for its nest in the hollows of these cacti. Its nest must be sheltered from the daytime sun and the nighttime cold, equally intense in the desert. Hidden in the cactus the bird watches for its prey, particularly insects. It will often attack reptiles, even little snakes, against which it is well armed with a hooked beak and sharp claws.

Another inhabitant of the cactus regions of the Southwest is the Gila or Saguaro Woodpecker, a bird which darts about in search of insects. It, too, hollows out nesting holes in the stems of the great saguaro cactus.

At certain times spring bushes and cacti are covered with brilliant multicolored flowers and the desert looks like a flower garden. This attracts many Hummingbirds which flit from flower to flower collecting the sweet nectar. They also collect a sweet liquid which flows from the wounds of cactus fruit when it has been damaged by chipmunks. Desert Hummingbirds are among the most beautiful of all, for their iridescent colors are often more brilliant than those of their relatives living in wet environments.

Many more birds have settled in the desert. Cactus Wrens, Mockingbirds, and Thrashers flit among the thorniest of plants with great agility, never colliding with the barbs which could prick them so easily. Flocks of small, plump Gambel's Quail run along the ground in Indian file, calling to each other in tuneful voices.

Birds of the desert lead a very special sort of life imposed on them by the heat and aridity. They hide during the day and take advantage of the cool morning and evening hours for their active life. Desert birds are not discouraged by the worst possible conditions but manage to draw on the few resources of their parched home.

Elf Owl

Gambel's Quail

Cactus Wren

Roadrunner

35

Lark

Sand Grouse

Courser

Bustard   Houbara

When a caravan stops at a resting place in the middle of the Sahara, around it is nothing but sand and pebbles. Dry and continuously swept by trade winds, the desert is bleak and inhospitable, so much so that the traveler is surprised at the appearance of several birds whose very existence in such a barren place seems miraculous.

For the small birds of the open desert one of the greatest problems is to find hiding places, for birds of prey are very common here and it is difficult for the victims to escape.

Luckily, the hunted have adopted an effective camouflage. Most desert birds sport a sand-colored or light gray plumage. Whether they are Larks, Sand Grouse, Coursers, or Bustards, their plumage enables them to blend effectively with the color of their surroundings. They are thus able to escape detection by the simplest of ways, for instance

crouching in a hole beside a stone. The Bustard is a fat bird which cannot fly well, but in addition to its coloring it can rely on its running ability to escape a pursuer's clutch. The little Lark, which also runs instead of hopping, prefers to bathe in dust rather than water. Nests of these birds are simply holes scooped out in the sand, perhaps at the base of a shrub.

Other birds in the Sahara have adopted an opposite technique in self-preservation. Some birds, like the Mourning Chat and the White-Rumped Black Chat, both cousins of the Wheatear, are vividly marked with black and white. When these birds are flying the pattern on their wings may be clearly seen. They are not edible, as they have a most unpleasant taste. They seem to warn possible attackers of this by their black and white markings which make it impossible to mistake them for more flavorful species. Color is their protection.

Birds of the Far North

THE Land of the Midnight Sun is one of the strangest places in the world. An icy desert in winter, it comes to life only when the snow melts in the valleys. Summer is brief and life seems more intense because the fine days are numbered. Flowers take only a few hours to grow and transform the landscape.

The cold waters of the region are rich with fish, and sea birds are the most numerous here. Among them are Gulls, Terns, Fulmars, Auks, and Murres. When their appetites are satisfied, these birds rest on the narrowest cliff ledges, and in spring Murres lay their pear-shaped eggs on the bare rocks without building nests. The pointed oval form of their eggs prevents them from rolling off; if dislodged, they spin around their pointed ends and thus remain

perfectly balanced even on a steeply sloping surface. Murres are extremely faithful to their breeding sites; they return to the same spot on the same cliff face year after year. At about two weeks old, the young flutter down and take to the sea in the company of their parents. Here they are safer from the attacks of marauding Gulls than they were in the bare cliff ledges where they were hatched.

As soon as the tundra lakes have melted, the Arctic Loons appear. The call of the Common Loon, a long, far-carrying, plaintive cry, is for all who have heard it the unforgettable sound of the northlands. The British call these birds Divers, for diving is their habitual method of feeding. They swim with ease, sometimes sinking up to their long, periscope-like necks in the water. They are clumsy,

Whooper Swan

Snowy Owl

Canada Goose

Red-Throated Loon

Red-Breasted Merganser

Ptarmigan

awkward movers on land, for their legs are set farther back on their bodies than are the legs of most birds. For this reason they must take off from the water rather than the land. They cover a great distance when doing so, but once airborne, they are excellent fliers, and can attain speeds of up to sixty miles an hour.

The Snowy Owls, great Owls with white feathers striped with black, feed on lemmings, small rodents which breed in large numbers in the Arctic. They are sometimes so numerous here that they look like tiny armies on the march, providing inviting feasts for these birds of prey. Since daylight is continuous above the Arctic Circle in summer, Snowy Owls are necessarily daylight hunters. Strong enough to kill arctic hares on the ground, they are fast and powerful enough fliers to kill Ducks on the wing.

But winter soon returns to the Far North. The cold drives the birds out of this now inhospitable land clothed in the polar night. Only the Ptarmigans remain, hollowing out dwellings for themselves in the thick white carpet where they live like Eskimos in igloos. They move about under the icy crust through galleries where they store berries and shoots under a thick layer of snow. Their pure white, winter feathers give them extra camouflage and render them invisible to animals who would eat them. Ptarmigans are unique in having completely feathered toes, very probably in order to enable them to walk in soft snow. They are a form of Grouse and when spring returns and the snow begins to melt, their plumage turns progressively brownish and grouselike in appearance, only the feathers of the legs and parts of the wings remaining white in summer.

Fulmar

Eider

Murre

Puffin

Razorbill

South American Birds

Condor

Rhea hunting in Argentina

WHEN the plundering conquistadors landed in South America, they were seeking gold and precious stones. Whether successful or not in their quest for material riches, they could not help observing the wonders of nature. Returning to Spain, they told tales of extraordinary animals and wonderful birds, for nowhere else in the world are birds so richly colored as in the lowland forests of the Amazon.

Dozens of different kinds of Hummingbirds sparkle like precious stones. Manakins, Cocks of the Rocks, Trogons, and Tanagers make colorful splashes in the forest. Tinamous can be heard conversing in pairs. The air rings with the strange call of the Cotinga and the grave voice of the Bellbird. But the most characteristic sounds of the forest are the harsh cries of Parrots. When hunting, they work in partnership with other birds, particularly Toucans, and even monkeys, so as to exploit together the resources of the forest. Little birds follow behind these hunters, eating insects disturbed by their movements.

Leaving the hot, wet lowlands and climbing the slopes of the Andes, one reaches the high plateaus, which, at sixteen thousand feet, make up the highest region in the world inhabited by man.

This is the country of the Condor, the bird king of the Andes, which has a wing span of up to ten feet. The Indians have made this bird a god, representing the spirit of the mountains, but nevertheless they capture these birds on certain occasions by very special methods. One of the most interesting methods consists of digging a ditch and covering it with branches on which an animal's carcass is placed. The hunter hides in the ditch and waits for a Condor to come and take the bait. While the bird has its attention on the food the hunter grasps it by the feet.

The Gauchos, or cowboys, of Argentina have a different method for hunting the Rhea, cousin of the Ostrich, a bird confined to the unforested parts of South America. Like the Ostrich, the Rhea cannot fly but is a very fast runner. These tough horsemen use bolas, fiber thongs weighted at one end with stones, which they whirl like lassos, throwing them at and entangling the birds' three-toed feet. The Toucan, along with the Hornbill, is credited as being the bird with the largest size of beak proportionate to body size. Most of the beak is hollow and not as heavy as it appears to be. Toucans are gregarious birds, are easily tamed and make delightful pets. Their flesh is eaten in South America.

Sun Parakeet

Quetzal

Scarlet Macaw

Toucan

Hoatzin

Hawaiian Birds

Akiapolaau

Iiwi

WHEN visiting the Pacific, the traveler is often amazed to realize that islands isolated from the rest of the world by hundreds of miles are inhabited by small birds many of which have at some time crossed the sea to reach these faraway places.

This is particularly noticeable in Hawaii, the newest of our fifty States. These volcanic islands are washed by sparkling tropic seas and have a variety of palms and semi-tropical flowering trees and plants. There are about 125 species of birds here, both migrant and resident. Among them are about sixty songbirds that are peculiar to Hawaii.

The moment a visitor arrives he will notice flocks of the well-known Frigate Birds, or Man-o'-War Birds. With their long, pointed wings and forked tails they fly with great ease, outlining graceful arcs and at times attaining speeds of well over one hundred miles an hour. They are dangerous plunderers and obtain much of their food by harassing other sea birds—Boobies, Pelicans, Cormorants, Terns, or Gulls—into dropping their catch. As soon as one of these birds has caught a fish and starts to take flight, the Frigate Bird falls on it. The victim tries by clever maneuvers to avoid its attacker, but it is seldom sufficiently agile and usually it drops its fish just in time to miss the Frigate's long, hooked beak. With great skill and keen eyesight, the Frigate Bird catches the fish before it hits the water. One might imagine a sort of agreement between Boobies and Frigate Birds, for a Frigate Bird will pursue

a Booby over the sea only and considers the latter to have won if it succeeds in reaching the shore. All the same, the Frigate Bird is a pirate. It was given its name by sailors who well knew those fast ships whose task it was to intercept the heavier commercial vessels. The male Frigate is a large, glossy black bird with a red pouch and long tail. The female is also black but its breast and sides are white.

Boobies seem to have a sense of social responsibility for if one of them is injured, members of the flock will care for and feed it until it is well. The Frigate has been observed to follow this practice as well. Boobies fly at an altitude of about fifty feet from where they will spy a school of fish, descend upon it like a sheet of rain, and scatter a wake of sea foam where they themselves have just clouded the sky. The Frigate, which robs them of their catch, is not their only enemy; crabs also steal their eggs.

The shores of Hawaii are inhabited by many other sea birds. Among them are the Noddy Terns with

Red-Footed Booby

brown, dusty feathers, and the Fairy Terns. The latter are very graceful birds with immaculate white feathers and seemingly transparent wings. Terns generally resemble Gulls but are smaller. Known also as Sea Swallows, they are a beautiful sight as they plummet headlong into the water in search of fish and small marine organisms.

Wandering along the shores, the bird watcher may see some of the last Hawaiian Geese or Nenes. These Nenes were once so much hunted that they almost became extinct, but they have survived through the rearing of a few pairs in captivity. Some of these Geese were released on the islands where they are at present protected. They are related to Brants but differ from them in the buff color of their necks, which are covered with long, pointed feathers.

The most interesting birds of the whole archipelago, or group of islands, are the Hawaiian Honeycreepers.

Their ancestors came here a long time ago, probably originating in America. As there was no competition they bred and gave rise to a number of different species which are significant in that they seem to be quite unrelated at the present time. In fact, if they did not all live in the same region we would be sure to class them in different families. The Honeycreepers'

Noddy Tern

Great Frigate Bird

Fairy Tern

development is a lesson in how birds may have become divided into such a multitude of species during the earth's development.

Some of the Honeycreepers, like the Koas and the Ous, have thick, strong beaks like little Parrots and feed on seeds, crushing the husks with ease. Others, such as the Akepas, have fine, pointed beaks, the mandibles slightly crossed at their tips. These they use to pry out insects from the bark and blossoms of certain trees.

41

Birds of the Antarctic

THE winds which sweep continually the island of South Georgia situated in the Atlantic, east of the southern tip of South America, are very violent. Only in the mornings do they abate slightly, and it is then that the huge Albatrosses can be seen flying in to rest on large tussock-covered sand dunes. These sea giants arrange their nests a certain distance from each other on the dunes in the form of pedestals made from collected vegetable rubbish,

moss, and roots. There the female lays her egg, which is about five and one quarter inches long, and sits on it for about seventy days. At the end of this period a big chick hatches out and the parents protect it from the cold for at least a month afterward. After this first month the chick looks like a huge ball of down. Its thick, furlike coat protects it from the cold, and the parents return only once a day to feed it by regurgitating a kind of pap. The young bird thrives

Albatrosses and their nests

42

on this and soon weighs approximately thirty pounds, which is more than its parents. It is as well that the parents then abandon the young Albatross completely, for it has to lose weight before it is able to fly. Its reserves are such that it can survive for more than three months without eating.

One by one the young Albatrosses fly off, first running along the ground, then lifting themselves slowly but gracefully like airplanes taking off from a long runway. Soon, like their parents, they become very skilled at flying, and at gliding, too, for without flapping their wings they are able to soar above the waves, taking advantage of the slightest puff of wind. They cover great distances across the Antarctic. Their migrations probably take them around the world several times before they return to their birthplaces.

When night falls on South Georgia Island, the darkness is suddenly enlivened with strange cries. They seem at first like the sounds of ghosts awakened by the twilight. They are the cries of Petrels. These sea birds are so well adapted to marine life that they can even drink sea water. They can assimilate quantities which would kill any other animal, eliminating the excess salt through special glands in the nostrils.

Petrels are mostly night birds. At nightfall they whirl into the sky and gather together, uttering shrill and regulated cries. Then they head for the sea to catch fish, crustaceans, and squid, which they eat in great quantities. The pattern of their lives can be understood from the fact that the sea creatures which they eat stay in the depths of the sea all day and rise to the surface only at night. Petrels are not confined to Antarctica; they are to be found off the coasts of every continent in the world.

During the day Petrels live in burrows built in the soft soil of the dunes. Each burrow consists of a tunnel about seven feet long leading to a spacious living room where the birds are well sheltered from rain and wind and enjoy a much warmer temperature than that outside. This is where they lay their eggs, which incubate for six or more weeks. The young Petrels, like the baby Albatrosses, must wait for their parents to come and feed them by regurgitating a predigested pap of sea creatures. They are safely out of reach of their enemies, in particular the large Skuas, which would immediately attack them if they left their burrows.

In this way the young Petrels grow and store up fat. In the past, people used to dislodge the fattened fledglings from their burrows and, by cooking them, extract a fat considered to be a great delicacy. This practice was common in Scotland; on Tristan da Cunha, an island in the mid-Atlantic between Africa and South America; and in South Australia.

Fortunately it has been stopped.

Giant Petrel

43

Australian Birds

A pair of Budgerigars

Australia has given us some of our most familiar cage birds, in particular the graceful Budgerigars or Parakeets. These birds are green in the natural state but by interbreeding man has modified the colors and produced beautiful chartreuse, white, blue-purple, and pale yellow birds. The pretty Budgerigar is a very popular indoor cage bird. It becomes a most engaging cage pet if given a lot of attention. It can become a good talker with a large vocabulary if it hears words repeated often enough. Most likely it doesn't really understand what it repeats but it is amusing to hear this bird speak. If several Budgerigars are kept together, or with other birds, they will not pick up words, but will imitate high-pitched bird sounds, which are easier for them to reproduce than the human voice.

ONE of the oddest and most magnificent birds of Australia is the Lyrebird. The name comes from the bird's long tail which when at rest resembles the form of this musical instrument. The two thick exterior feathers look like the wood of the lyre while the inside feathers are finer and long and slender like the instrument's strings. The lyre-shaped tail is characteristic only of the male. It is used not as a means to make music but in order to attract a mate, for whom the male promenades in majestic poses, opening and closing the rich tail feathers, which can be folded up over the back. This gorgeous bird can imitate about fifteen different kinds of birds whose voices it has heard in the forest.

Throughout the Australian bush a curious laughing sound can be heard. It is the language of the Laughing Jackass which still keeps its aboriginal name of Kookaburra. About the size of a Magpie, this bird has a strange, ringing cry rather like a rude human laugh, which it utters with great regularity at dawn and dusk. The Laughing Jackass is often seen beside water, but it is actually a land bird. To fish it prefers lizards, insects, and even young chickens which it steals from farmyards.

Laughing Jackass

Lyrebird

HOW DO BIRDS LIVE?

A MAN can survive for several weeks without eating, for his body has reserves which enable him to survive. Some birds come under this category, too. An Eagle can fast for nearly a month without suffering seriously, and a Hen for about ten days. However, most birds die after going without food for only a little time. Bengalees and many other small birds die just a few hours after their digestive tracts have been emptied.

Birds are extremely active creatures. Whereas the normal human heart beats seventy times a minute, the Duck's heart beats two hundred times, the Hen's heart 312 times, and that of the Sparrow 460 times! Heart beats of small birds can exceed one thousand per minute in flight. If we took a bird's temperature we would think it was feverish. As an example, the thermometer would indicate a normal 113 degrees Fahrenheit for the Robin and the Sparrow Hawk. Matching the efficiency of this system is the rate of food consumption which may be eighty per cent of the body weight daily.

This can be explained by comparing a living creature to an automobile. The faster the car is driven, the more gasoline and oil it uses. Birds are rather like high-speed cars. A great amount of energy is needed for flying and for other activities.

A bird must therefore eat very frequently. Before dawn birds begin looking for food, and they do not rest until sunset, as a huge quantity of food is necessary to satisfy their seldom contented appetites. Each day a Warbler eats its weight in insects. Gannets and Cormorants can eat from four to seven pounds of fish daily, the equivalent of their own weight. Sandpipers, which search so avidly for little sea creatures, also need to eat their own weight in food. Hummingbirds feed chiefly on nectar from flowers and may take in every day an amount equal to twice their weight.

A bird spends most of its life looking for food, though the urgency of the search is not the same for all species. Birds of prey, whose opportunities for feeding are necessarily haphazard, go without eating on some days, just as lions do. Shrikes think of the future and store some of their victims, grasshoppers or small lizards, by hanging them on the thorns of trees. Some Woodpeckers make holes in trees where they hide seeds which they feed on later. These pantries are very welcome in days of need. Most other birds, however, live from day to day. The daily success of their hunting and gathering is a matter of life and death for each one of them.

The length of a bird's life varies. Birds in captivity have been known to attain the following ages: an Owl, sixty-eight, an Eagle, fifty-five, a Condor, fifty-two, and a Pelican, fifty-one years. There have been the cases of a Cardinal thirty years old, a Sparrow of twenty-three and a Canary of twenty-two—all caged birds.

Barn Swallow

Insect Hunters

Honey Buzzard

LET us imagine that we could count every land animal in the world. Insects would far outnumber any other kind because of the unbelievable rate at which they multiply. Their eggs are laid by the millions and their generations succeed one another very rapidly. The world would be a seething mass of insects if they were not hunted by other animals who reduce their numbers.

Some insects are useful, but many others are very harmful, particularly to crops and harvests. Nature has provided ways of combating this constant menace, and birds are in the front line of defense. Entomologists have estimated that the annual loss of crops in the United States must run into hundreds of millions of dollars. However, these losses would be very many times greater without the insect-eating birds which destroy huge quantities of harmful insects. In general, a bird eats several hundred insects at a single meal, and sometimes several thousand if the insects are small. It has been calculated that in a two-hundred-acre field in North Carolina, birds daily destroy a million green bugs or wheat aphids, insects which are very harmful to crops.

Some night flyers are great eaters. Nighthawks catch their food on the wing. Examination has shown that a single bird has eaten as many as three thousand mosquitoes, as well as many other insects, for a meal. A Swainson's Hawk may eat as many as one hundred grasshoppers for lunch. A family of Tits eats up to fourteen million insects in a single year.

Cuckoos are avid eaters of caterpillars, which they prefer to any other prey. Many of these larvae are covered with long stinging hairs which frighten off most other birds. Over three hundred caterpillars have been found in the stomach of a single Cuckoo.

Every crop pest has many enemies. In the United States the alfalfa weevil is sought by forty-five different birds, the cotton boll weevil is the food of sixty-six, the chestnut weevil of sixty-four, the clover root borer of eighty-five, the gypsy moth of forty-six, the potato beetle of twenty-five, and the wireworm of one hundred and sixty-eight birds!

Insects are hunted everywhere; there is no refuge where they can escape from birds. Among the cleverest birds is the Swallow which chases its winged victims in flight. Swallows dive with open beaks upon their prey of mosquitoes, small flies, dragonflies, and tiny butterflies.

As many as sixty-eight cotton boll weevils have been found in the stomach of a Swallow.

Insects which are hunted on land and in the air try to hide in the bark or branches of trees, but even in the trunk itself they are not safe from the cunning Woodpeckers. These birds find them with their beaks which work with the efficiency and rhythm of pneumatic drills. As soon as an insect or larva is partly

Green Woodpecker

Yellow-Billed Cuckoo

Flicker

Hoopoe

exposed, the bird picks it out with its long tongue, which can stretch as far as four inches from its beak. This supple tongue, coated with a slimy liquid, often has backward-pointing spines at the end so that the Woodpecker can easily extract a larva from its covering by attaching it to the end of its tongue.

Woodpeckers are often blamed for making holes in trees and weakening them, and for leaving the way clear for parasitic fungi, but the benefit the tree derives from being rid of insects is far greater than the damage it suffers in the course of the operation.

There are over twenty species of Woodpeckers in the United States and Canada. Most of them live in holes in trees and feed on grubs found in the bark. One of the best-known, the loud-voiced Flicker, feeds on the ground. More than five thousand ants have been found in the stomach of a single Flicker.

Other birds hunt for insects among the leaves of trees. This is the difficult task of the many Warblers which in the spring attack their victims in the green branches. Flycatchers, Phoebes, Kingbirds, and some birds of prey pursue them on the wing.

47

Towhee

Evening Grosbeak

A FLOCK of birds has come to rest in a large fir tree, brightening the dark green leaves with red and yellow patches. Their beaks are extraordinary. Instead of ending in a point or a hook, as do those of other birds, the two mandibles of the beak are actually crossed at the tips either to the left or right. These birds are Crossbills, distant cousins of the Finches. They specialize in collecting seeds of fir trees, particularly of the Norway spruce. Their beaks are so shaped to form a perfect tool for extracting seeds hidden between the scales of fir cones. They received their name because of the overlapping tips of their bills.

Crossbills skillfully divide the cones, using their beaks as powerful levers. They scoop out the seeds of a cone with a spoon-like tongue, but they are wasteful feeders for they will throw away a fir cone before they have extracted all the seeds. These operations are never carried out alone, for Crossbills like company and move in great flocks over huge areas of North America, continuing on their journeys each year as

soon as the young are able to fly. These birds are found in almost all coniferous forests from Alaska to Michigan.

When we want to eat a nut we use a nutcracker to break the shell. Grosbeaks have an advantage over us in that they have built-in nutcrackers. These sturdy birds, no bigger than Finches, have very strong beaks worked by powerful muscles. Capable of exerting a pressure of about 110 pounds, their beaks easily break the hardest fruit stones to extract the kernel. Their food, which no other bird lays claim to, consists of various seeds, from blackthorn and hawthorn berries to the fruits of the maple and the ash. Even when eating cherries, Grosbeaks throw away the sweet pulp and eat only the kernel inside the stone. Their diet allows them to stay in cold climates when winter has emptied the pantries of other birds. The commonest Grosbeaks in America are the Rose-Breasted Grosbeak, a brilliant singer; the Black-Headed Grosbeak in the Rocky Mountain region; and the Pine Grosbeak, a winter visitor from the subarctic forests.

The feeding habits of the North American Towhee reveal how varied a bird's diet can be. About the size

Crossbill

48

Seed Eaters

White-Throated Sparrow

Yellowhammer

of a small Blackbird, the Towhee scratches with its feet among the dead leaves, making a noise like a squirrel, out of all proportion to its size. An eater of wild fruit of all sorts, especially berries, it also eats ants, larvae, and insects. The Towhee is very helpful to agriculture, because it prevents weeds from spreading by eating their seeds.

Seeds are the staple diet of many birds. Even when seeds have many hard coverings, birds can crush them without difficulty. Among the biggest eaters of seeds are the Sparrows, so common and diversified in North America. At first glance they all look alike with brown and gray striped feathers. But on closer observation they can be seen to be divided into many different species distinguishable by the colors of their heads, which are marked with either white, chestnut or yellow patches. Each kind has its favorite haunt, but the species as a whole prefers open plains, fields, and meadows, settings where their coloring makes them indistinguishable from the surroundings. The House Sparrow is considered a pest not only because it eats fruit buds and garden produce and drives away helpful insect-eating birds, but because it makes war on the small native birds of an area.

Berries are the favorite food of many birds. Mountain ashes, hawthorns, and elders are very tempting for the European cousin of our Wood Thrush, the Mistle Thrush, whose feathers are marked with dark speckles. The grapes of autumn seem to attract these harvesters, which otherwise eat insects, butterflies, caterpillars, not to mention slugs and snails which they cleverly extract from their shells by breaking them on a stone.

In the winter the Mistle Thrush changes his diet to mistletoe berries. Mistletoe stays green the year round. From autumn on it is covered with little white berries containing a blackish kernel. The gelatinous white substance is much appreciated by the Mistle Thrush which swallows the whole berry as we would an oyster. Swallowed with the pulp, the seed passes through the digestive system and yet retains its ability to germinate. When a Mistle Thrush excretes the seed on a branch, it sticks to the bark and starts a new mistletoe plant. As the plant feeds the bird and the bird scatters the seed, this is another example of a mutually beneficial relationship in nature.

Mistle Thrush

Birds of Prey

Peregrine Falcon plunging

BIRDS of prey have a bad reputation. They are blamed for causing damage in farmyards and inflicting losses among game birds. They are also accused of cruelty. But these are hasty judgments and the case against carnivorous birds should be revised. What is more, their numbers are decreasing at such a rate that these birds can scarcely be called harmful anywhere today.

We admire their noble appearance. Among our handsomest birds is the Duck Hawk, named in Europe the Peregrine Falcon. This bird may be seen on the seashore and inland, particularly in regions of high cliffs and even at times on city buildings. Easily recognized by its long, tapering wings and elegant outline, it is the biggest Hawk of its kind and also the fastest. Its favorite prey is other birds, Pigeons, Crows, Gulls, and even little Sparrows. As soon as it is within range of its victim, the Duck Hawk spirals up into the sky and then falls on its target in a spectacular dive. With its wings folded back along its body, resembling a jet aircraft, it reaches a speed of 120 miles an hour in a vertical dive. It seizes the prey in its feet equipped with sharp claws and beats it to death against its sturdy chest. It never picks the prey up in its beak.

Other birds of prey hunt by lying in wait to spot their victims on the ground. The Buzzard or Vulture perches on a tree or post looking out for possible victims, for the most part small rodents. In helping to reduce the numbers of these harmful animals, Buzzards are beneficial.

When night falls on the countryside, most birds retire to their sleeping quarters, both the hunters and the hunted. Owls come out of their daytime hiding places to search for food. These night birds have been hunted down by man since the earliest times as creatures of the devil, probably because of their nocturnal habits and mournful cries. Yet with few exceptions Owls are not only inoffensive creatures but are very beautiful, with big golden eyes opening in the center of a rufflike circle of feathers. Their silky feathers feel like velvet, each having thousands of filaments, enabling the Owls to glide silently through the calm night air. Their hearing is acute and their eyesight is amazingly well developed. The tufts of feathers or "horns" are characteristic in many species. Their field of vision, smaller than that of daytime

Barn Owl

birds of prey, would be a disadvantage to Owls if it were not for the fact that these birds can turn their heads through an angle of 270 degrees, almost a complete circle. Owls hunt small rodents, voles, and field mice, nearly all of them nocturnal animals. The Barn Owl and the Tawny Owl may consume as many as six or seven thousand small animals a year. Rodents are swallowed whole. Then the digestive juices do their work and the carnivorous bird simply casts out the

hair and bones in the form of pellets. An analysis of these pellets shows the ornithologist exactly what an Owl has eaten.

The living places of Owls vary from prairies and marshes to dense forests. Their abundance in any locality is in proportion to their prey. They have even been known to live in the heart of large cities. Owls exist throughout the world, except in parts of Polynesia. Over 325 types have been recorded.

51

Fish Eaters

Osprey

Gannet diving

IMAGINE taking a ride in a boat on a river winding between two rows of trees and bushes. At every bend a different view of the countryside is to be seen. Suddenly a bird bigger than a Robin, with blue-gray feathers on its back, and white neck and breast, darts swiftly by. This short-tailed bird with a sharp beak and ragged crest is a Belted Kingfisher. If we keep very quiet it will return and perch on a branch overhanging the river to watch for fish. We may see it fly along the river, stop, flap its wings over a certain spot, then suddenly dive and catch an unwary fish swimming near the surface. Sometimes it will spear the fish on the end of its sharp, pointed beak, but more often it will seize it between its mandibles. Finding a quiet place, it will swallow its catch head first so that the fish passes more easily down its throat.

These elegant birds are often accused of reducing the number of game fish by killing the young ones. However this accusation is unfair, for the Kingfisher usually eats minnows, chub, and shallow-water fish which are not sought by fishermen. Their diet is supplemented by water insects, small frogs, tadpoles, and some crustaceans.

The Europeans have another Kingfisher, smaller than ours, but more brightly colored. It has an azure blue back, contrasting sharply with its vivid russet belly. A legend tells how the Kingfisher became so gaily colored. Long ago, it wanted to reach the sun, and its underparts were scorched while its back absorbed the color of the sky. This daring, legendary venture had happy consequences, for it gave Europe one of its most beautiful birds.

Many other fishers have settled beside fresh water. The Great Blue Herons, the biggest of all Herons, stand on long legs scouring the shallow waters step by step in search of fish. With a brisk straightening

Black-Crowned
Night Heron

52

of the neck they harpoon their prey with the end of their dagger-like beaks. Their cousins, the Black-Crowned Night Herons, prefer to fish at night. They spend the day quietly hidden in thickets or reeds and at twilight emerge, making strange croaking sounds, to fish in ponds and marshes.

Some birds of prey specialize in fishing. The Osprey falls like a stone from the sky onto a fish swimming near the surface and seizes its prey with its sharp claws. After hitting the water with a tremendous splash, sometimes disappearing in a cloud of spray, the Osprey takes to flight, prey in its talons. Frequently Ospreys are themselves pursued by the bigger and more skilled Bald Eagles, which steal from them their newly caught prizes. Where they are unmolested, Ospreys become tame and will occupy the same nest year after year.

Kingfishers, Ospreys, and Herons are lake and stream birds. In an earlier chapter we discussed the sea birds, each of which has a specialized fishing technique. There are great numbers of sea birds, as the riches of the ocean provide the largest source of life in the world.

Belted Kingfisher

European Kingfisher

53

Carrion Eaters

African Vultures

Vultures feeding on lions' kill

IN tropical Africa the Savannah grasslands seem to be sleeping in the noonday sun. There is not a bird in the deep blue sky until suddenly a majestic figure veers into sight. Without flapping its wings a Vulture wheels in ever decreasing circles. A second and then a third come to join in the pattern. Soon a large group of these peculiar birds of prey is flying slow circles in the overheated air. Why are they circling? Some lions must have just made a kill, which the first Vulture spotted. Its companions saw it wheeling and have come because they know that a meal is assured them if they wait.

The lions will be the first served, and they are already attending the grisly feast. Around them

Marabou

prowl hyenas and jackals, which come to share in the repast. When the lions eventually go to sleep under the acacia trees, they leave one of their number as guard over the dismembered victim but later he, too, retires, overcome with the sleep which follows a hearty meal.

Now the Vultures alight, one by one. In flight, these graceful birds are most impressive. Once on the ground, however, they inspire nothing but disgust. Their strong beaks tear apart the prey which they are too weak to catch in their relatively feeble claws. Their featherless necks, their massiveness, and their endless squabbling add to their awkward and undignified appearance.

The Vultures' ability to discover food is one of the

Griffon Vulture

perplexing problems in ornithology. They can find decaying meat even though the food is hidden from view and their sense of smell is not regarded as being keen. It is likely that both sight and smell play a role in the discovery of food, with sight predominating.

Vultures play an important part in cleaning up debris. These scavengers of the tropical bush clear it of carcasses which, if left untouched, would decay and pollute the surroundings.

For this reason Vultures are welcome in the tropics. They are allowed to live in villages and even near towns. There is no African village without its carrion eaters, and Vultures are often helped in their task by Kites and Marabou Storks. In India, Africa, and tropical America, Vultures may be found wher-

ever scavengers are needed. This clean-up work is extremely useful in maintaining sanitary conditions and helping prevent tropical epidemics.

But we do not need to go to Africa or India to see Vultures. In the southern states, towns and streets are frequented by Black Vultures which are found wherever there is something to eat. Valuable scavengers, they are protected by law. These Vultures are esteemed throughout America's semi-tropical regions for the services they render to man. Vultures are found wherever there is food within their range.

The Vulture does not have a nest but lays its one to three eggs under logs or stumps, on the ground, in caves, or similar places. The young Vultures are born naked and are fed by regurgitation.

Hummingbirds

Magnificent Hummingbird

Black-Fronted Hummingbird

IF there were a beauty prize for birds it would undoubtedly be awarded to the Hummingbirds. These natives of the New World are nature's fire-flashing jewels. Their plumage is so brilliant that naturalists have given them the names of precious stones: Ruby-Throated Hummingbird, Amethyst-Throated Hummingbird, Fork-Tailed Emerald. The brilliance of their feathers is produced by each barbule which breaks up the light like a prism. The most detailed chemical analysis of their feathers shows nothing but black pigment, which means that the color of these birds is a wonderful trick of the light.

Hummingbirds are our smallest birds, and some of them are no larger than an insect, weighing about one-fourteenth of an ounce. Yet this minute bird has the same parts of the body as any other bird: a heart, a stomach, and a liver which function normally.

Despite their tiny size Hummingbirds are noted for their fearlessness and pugnacity. They adjust to people easily and even enter houses. If a Hummingbird is disturbed by a predatory bird such as a Crow, Hawk, or Eagle it will make an attack.

Hummingbirds have a special, vibrant way of flying, which produces a buzzing sound similar to that of bumblebees. Their wings beat about fifty times a second, thus becoming invisible to our eyes. They are the only birds which can hover on the spot and can fly backward as easily as forward.

This unique method of flight allows them to draw from flowers the precious nectar which they collect as avidly as any insect. The sweet liquid held in brilliantly colored flowers is pumped down by their very long tongues. The sides of the tongue are curved up to make a tube which the bird plunges into the flowers' hearts. Hummingbirds enjoy real nectar revelries, but they complete their diet with many kinds of insects.

Their choice of food permits them to inhabit both North and South America. They are most common in the hot, wet forests of the Amazon, but they also live in the high plateaus of the Andes, the arid Mexican deserts, and even the forests of Canada and Alaska. This wide variety of habitat indicates the remarkable hardiness of these birds, which is amazing considering their size.

Swallow-Tailed
Hummingbird

Sickle-Billed
Hummingbird

Topaz Hummingbird

Racquet-Tailed
Hummingbird

Star-Throat
Hummingbird

Broad-Tailed
Hummingbird

Sword-Billed
Hummingbird

The Honey Guide

Honey Guide

Ratel or
Honey Badger

THE African brush echoes with a curious sound, like the shaking of a half-empty matchbox. At a first glance we hardly notice the bird that makes this noise. It is about the size of a Lark or a Sparrow, and is called a Honey Guide. If we approach it, the bird will repeat its strange cry, showing off its white-trimmed tail as if to draw our attention. Then it flies off and perches about thirty yards away, repeating its curious behavior. If we follow it, the Honey Guide leads us through the forest until we reach a tree around which the bird flutters. If we look carefully, we will soon see what the bird was leading us to—a hive of wild bees in a tree, in an old stump, or even in the ground. The aim of the bird's repeated actions is to persuade us to break open the hive. It watches us and when we have finished and departed it will come and treat itself to its favorite food, not the honey or the bees, but the wax of which the honeycomb is made.

This is an interesting example of cooperation between man and bird, well known to all Africans. Men seeking honey willingly follow the bird to discover the way to the hive. Once the honey has been removed, the bird enjoys the wax. Digesting this wax is too much of a problem for other stomachs and one that seems only partially solved by these Honey Guides. Ornithologists are still puzzled by the role of wax in the diet of these friendly birds, and the means by which they digest it.

Not only does the Honey Guide profit by enjoying the wax which man has made available for it, but it also obtains the insect grubs from the fragments left behind.

Before man existed in Africa, how did the Honey Guide manage? It used various wild mammals, especially the ratel, or honey badger, whose services it still employs whenever an opportunity arises. This cousin of our badger, which is about the same size, loves honey and bees' eggs, so it follows the bird to the hive. The ratel upsets the hive and licks up the sweet liquid in spite of the bees, against whose attacks it is protected by a thick hide. The bird waits patiently and then helps itself to the wax.

THE BREEDING HABITS OF BIRDS

THE return of spring can be observed in many ways. Buds open, hedges are green again, a warm breeze chases frost from the valleys, and birds begin to sing.

After the migrants depart in large flocks in the fall, the birds who remain at home join together, as if to help one another. Some come close to our houses and others leave the snow-covered woods where food was scarce for the fields where there are the remains of grain, or for the hedges where there are still some berries and insects.

From the very first days of spring the habits of birds begin to change. Community life ceases to be important and birds begin to feel more independent. They shun the company of others and they chase off any birds which try to come near. Every male takes charge of a territory which he claims as his own, and he forbids other birds to enter it, sometimes becoming involved in violent fights. Dressed in a showy costume, the male bird struts around his property. In a loud voice he proclaims his ownership of the piece of field, or hedge, or tree he has chosen.

But a bird does not wish to be entirely alone on his property so he searches for a mate as soon as possible. His song and his dress announce loudly that he is a bachelor with attractive property, looking for a suitable mate. So that he may mate, nature provides him with a coat of far more vivid and striking colors than he will have during the rest of the year. The female, so humble in appearance compared to the dazzling male, cannot help but be impressed.

Some birds, however, are sociable the year around, including the mating season. Sea birds fall into this category and nest only in huge colonies. Perhaps the reason is that the sea offers its birds inexhaustible resources. Land birds do not find food so easily, therefore they are forced to spread out over the countryside and live in families apart from each other.

To win a mate, the male Black-Crowned Heron presents his chosen female with twigs, one at a time. Sometimes she not only responds to his suggestions but also starts to hunt for twigs herself and then builds a nest in which the pair can raise a brood of young. To attract a mate the male Tern catches a little fish and parades with it up and down the beach. When a female Tern comes to him and takes the fish, he bows and scrapes the sand before her, keeping alert for any signs of cooperation. If his suit is successful, he proceeds after mating to prepare a hole in the sand in which she makes the nest.

The spring is the busiest time of the year for all birds for it is then that they must find a mate, lay their eggs, and, after the eggs are hatched, spend night and day feeding and bringing up the young.

Bird Song

Song Sparrow

DURING a walk in woods and fields we may be disappointed at first. We have studied in detail the colors of birds and can tell one kind from another by their plumage, but it is not easy to see birds in their natural state except for a brief moment when one peeps through the leaves or flashes across our path.

Luckily their song is as characteristic of birds as is their coloring and the shape of their beaks. Each of the many Warblers has a characteristic song by which it may be recognized, even when it is hidden in the leaves. Their songs vary in pitch, volume, and quality. Some Warblers have only weak, trilling songs, but some, like the Yellow Warbler and the Yellow-Throated Warbler, have real vocal ability.

A stream of short notes may ring from a low bush— not very tuneful notes, but tumbling one after the other as if the bird were angry. This is the song of the House Wren, whose tiny size seems out of all proportion to the noise it makes.

The best singer among the Sparrows is the Song Sparrow which will perch on a high branch, lift its head to the sky, and then sing about a dozen notes, grouped in various ways. Each bird has five or six songs, each lasting two or three seconds; when the bird is excited it will repeat its program about ten times a minute.

The Cardinal which enlivens the countryside with its scarlet clothes also charms us with its pleasant voice. Its tuneful song consists of whistled phrases with varied intonations. Whistling is also a specialty of Grackles and particularly of Baltimore Orioles, which warn each other of the approach of danger with prolonged whistling. Although their song consists of only a few notes they can modify their intonation to an astonishing extent.

There are many beautiful singers among our birds. A prize should certainly go to the Hermit Thrush which likes the damp, dark interior of woods. Smaller than a Robin, this Thrush is modestly colored, as are most good songsters. The limpid, lyrical richness of its song is difficult to describe. It begins with a phrase of linked notes rising and descending. Then the theme is repeated at an ever higher and higher pitch, the volume changing as well as the notes. The song is

Hermit Thrush

often sung in the evening or at night and the bird has received the name of "Swamp Angel."

The European Nightingale also exemplifies vocal art. The purity and unequaled variety of its song justify its reputation. However, in the opinion of those people who are familiar with the songs of both birds, it is the American Hermit Thrush which is considered the more vocally gifted.

Some birds seem to lack the imagination to find a characteristic tune, and so they imitate the songs of other birds. The most familiar of these imitators is the Mockingbird, the size of a Robin, with light gray feathers and white spots on wings and tail which make it easy to spot when in flight. These comic creatures can reproduce almost any song they hear, including the "Cock-a-doodle doo" of the

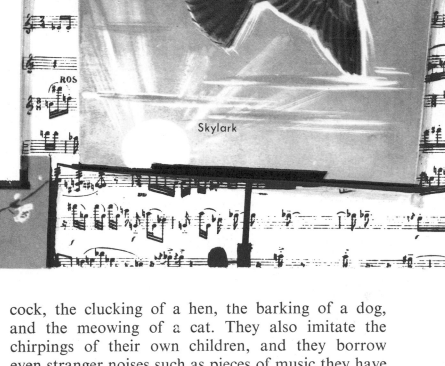

Skylark

Serin

Nightingale

cock, the clucking of a hen, the barking of a dog, and the meowing of a cat. They also imitate the chirpings of their own children, and they borrow even stranger noises such as pieces of music they have happened to hear. A member of their family, the Catbird, whose call could easily be confused with the meowing of a cat, also has this imitative gift.

Another bird with talent for imitation is the Starling, whose infinitely varying song reproduces many sounds of modern life. There is the story of an Englishman who, while busy cutting his lawn, was constantly bothered by the ringing of the telephone. Each time he stopped work and rushed into the house, and each time there was no one on the line. Looking around he realized that it was a teasing Starling who was giving perfect imitations of a telephone bell.

We must not forget all the other, less harmonious songs—the cawing of Crows, the trumpet blast of the Heron, the quacking of Ducks, and the moaning of Bitterns in the distant marshes. The call of the Bittern is like the noise made by an old pump which has run dry.

All these sounds are made by birds to attract a mate, to whom the noises seem as pleasant as a sweet serenade.

The elaborate variety of their songs is due to the complex muscle arrangement of birds' lungs and throats. There are so many kinds of songbirds that the order to which they belong makes up more than half of the world's bird species.

Courting Displays

Capercaillie (cock and hen)

Ruffs in courtship display

WHAT would we think of a young man who called on his fiancée without bothering to dress up? This is a mistake which birds never make, for they are at their most beautiful when courting. Their plumage is arranged to help them attract mates as quickly as possible.

We see this in the farmyard. The Turkey struts before the modestly dressed female, spreading out his tail feathers for her to admire. In the park the Peacock unfolds his fan-like tail, decorated with a thousand eyes, and each feather vibrates as the Peahen approaches.

Not all birds are so richly dressed, but they all draw attention to some aspect of their plumage, however humble it may be. In the spring watch the English Sparrow in the parks. The males, easily recognizable by their black bibs, strut in front of their brown mates. They dance, spreading out their tails and puffing out their black throats which they thrust forward. "Look how handsome I am. Look at my feathers all striped with black, brown, and white," they seem to say, until the female replies, "What a handsome partner! I would be proud to have such a finely dressed mate!"

The ceremonies of courtship are most complicated among the brilliantly dressed birds. Multicolored Pheasants spread out their tails and ruffs and unfold their wings to display their splendor. Herons bristle up their chest feathers which grow at the time of courtship. Egrets unfurl the long silky feathers on their backs, the feathers which were once so much sought after by women to wear in their hats.

All this takes place in the midst of a concert of song, particularly among the duller-colored birds, which seem to make up in song what they lack in color.

There are other customs of courtship. Terns present their mates with a little fish held at the end of the

Greater Prairie Chicken

beak, just as a young man might offer a box of chocolates. Often the spouse accepts the gift which sometimes causes an ill-timed quarrel, each bird wanting to eat the so-called present.

Among shore birds, the Ruffs of the Old World form companies to do their courting. When they arrive in Holland and Scandinavia where they bring up their young, they acquire a strange ruff of long feathers, like a shield covering their chests. The males gather in a field and unfurl their ruffs, bristling up the feathers. Getting more and more worked up, they fall on one another like knights in the jousts of the Middle Ages. These duels, in which there is neither victor nor vanquished, allow the birds to show themselves off to the Reeves, as their mates are called.

The most curious displays are those of the Prairie Chickens which take place every year in the great plains of the western United States. In April the males gather in bands of up to four hundred birds. The ceremony begins at dawn. Each bird raises its tail like a fan of rigid, spread-out feathers. It puffs up the bright orange pouches on its chest, then, running to and fro, it throws these pouches forward, at the same time jerking its neck sharply back. This is accompanied by hollow cries which can be heard as much as two hundred yards away from the ceremony. These very special dances were noticed long ago by the American Indians who copied them and on certain occasions performed dances, every movement of which recalled exactly those of the birds.

Great Crested Grebe

Birds of Paradise

Superb Bird of Paradise

King of Saxony Bird of Paradise

Enameled Bird of Paradise

GREAT excitement stirred the Spanish court of the sixteenth-century Emperor Charles V when the expedition of the explorer Magellan returned from its voyage around the world. Magellan himself had died in the course of the journey but the returning survivors told of many wonderful things, including an account of fairy tale birds. These birds, the sailors reported, had no feet or wings, but instead had long tufts of silky feathers. Since the ground seemed too unworthy a place for such delicate creatures, they could have come only from heaven. So the sailors called them Birds of Paradise.

Science has since disproved these fanciful suppositions. We now know that when skinning these birds of their feathers, the natives had removed the feet which they evidently considered useless. Birds of Paradise, of course, do not come from heaven but live in the dense forests of New Guinea and North Australia.

These birds are the most beautiful of the feathered world. Papuan chieftains chose their feathers as the insignia of their rank. Later, as knowledge of these wonderful birds spread, their feathers were exported to decorate the heads of Indian Maharajas. Before long they reached Europe, where dandies quarreled over them for huge sums of gold. Today the feathers are no longer used for decorative purposes, as it has

become illegal to kill a Bird of Paradise. Birds of Paradise always look magnificent, but as with all birds the males look their best when they are courting. The females are more soberly dressed, as if gay clothes did not go together with the life of a wife and mother.

If we were to go deep into the damp forests on the mountain slopes of Papua, we might witness one of the most wonderful sights of nature. We would see Birds of Paradise gathered in groups of about twelve to a tree. They might be one of a number of kinds, the most amazing of which is the Blue Bird of Paradise. This bird has beautiful azure blue ornamental feathers. To display them, it hangs head down and swings to and fro in a graceful, circular motion. Another, the Greater Bird of Paradise, goes through a series of complicated rituals in which it lowers its head while displaying the long, silky side feathers of its tail. The Sickle Bill, the biggest of all Birds of Paradise, is so elaborate that it seems to have four wings. It displays its wings by raising them while simultaneously opening its beak to show the bright yellow inside. The Superb Birds of Paradise have a huge ruff and a frill of bright green feathers, widely spread out when courting, to show off their splendor.

The rituals of the Bowerbirds are even stranger than

Bowerbird

Six-Plumed Bird of Paradise

female

Greater Bird of Paradise, male

Blue Bird of Paradise

Long-Tailed Bird of Paradise

those of their cousins, the Birds of Paradise. They also live in the dense Papuan forests. These birds make up for the relative modesty of their feathers with extraordinary refinements in their courting technique. The males place twigs in the ground in the form of quite a large bower or stall. The ground all around is carefully cleared to form a sort of arena which they decorate with flowers, berries, feathers, and even pieces of plates and dishes stolen from neighboring encampments. When this work is finished, the female bird perches in a nearby tree. Then the male bird begins to dance inside his construction, coming out to take up strange postures. He picks up an object in his beak as if to win his mate's admiration, then replaces it and continues his curious behavior. His special courting display makes the Bowerbird one of the most extraordinary suitors of the feathered world.

Other species of the Bowerbird build very elaborate parks or bowers in which they erect one or more structures. The Golden Bowerbird builds a large hut piled up around the base of a small tree, sometimes to the height of six feet, and then builds around it a number of smaller hut-like structures. The whole group together looks like a miniature native encampment, a most elaborate system with which to woo a mate.

65

Nests and Nesting

WE have developed infinite varieties of dwellings, from the shepherd's humble cottage to the gigantic skyscraper. The site and the climate in which we are building invariably have an influence.

But with birds it is different. Each little builder has to find a technique to suit its strength, the area where it is building and the materials at its disposal. Without being taught, a bird will always construct its nest in a style peculiar to its own species. Instinct plays an important part, as can be observed by studying the nesting habits of birds in captivity. A bird which has never known its parents nor watched them build a nest will, when it grows up, build a nest of a kind its species has always built.

Nests are constructed and located for the protection of eggs and young, being built in secret places away from enemies. Albatrosses place their nests on remote islands; Eagles and Hawks have their nests high up on cliffs or in trees; songbirds conceal their nests on the ground or in trees. Shore birds with protectively colored eggs simply scoop out a place on the ground. Since it is the female who generally builds the nest, it is she who is colored so as to resemble the natural background.

Some birds do not bother with complicated plans. Murres, as we have seen, do not even trouble to collect bits of seaweed, but lay their large, pear-shaped eggs on the bare rock of the narrow ledges where they nest. Plovers do not require a nest either; just a dip in the ground will do for them. Here, their protectively colored eggs are much better hidden than if the parent birds had built a complicated nest. What use would the young birds have for a nest, since they can run as soon as they hatch from the egg? They run in order to feed and take shelter.

The Lark nests on the ground, too, hiding her nest among stones which shelter it from the sun. As her young will be weak and naked on hatching, she has to build a dome of twigs to shelter her fragile brood.

In the Middle Ages barons surrounded their castles with moats filled with water, so that their enemies could not reach them. This is what the Grebe does. It builds a floating nest on the surface of ponds. First, it collects water plants and builds a platform. Then it moors this platform to some reeds. In the event of a sudden rise in the water level, the platform can slide up and down on the reeds. Thus the nest is virtually unsinkable and the precious eggs are kept safe from flooding.

Some land birds have no enemies, at least not around their nests. Who could oust Crows from their nests in the swaying branches high up in the poplars?

Rooks in their rookery

Storks in their nest

Screech Owl with young

Murre with its egg

Nest of the American Redstart

Although Storks' nests on the roofs of houses may be seen from far away, they are quite safe from attack; it is impossible for cats and rats to reach them.

Nesting is a much greater problem for other birds, especially for small ones, whose newly hatched young are naked and unable to stand on their feet. These babies can only open their mouths wide for constant feeding by the parents, who must leave their nests unprotected while they hunt all day long to satisfy their brood. A warm, soft, and well-hidden nest in the branches is essential to protect the baby birds from the cold and the other enemies that would otherwise soon kill them. The Red-Eyed Vireo builds a finely plaited cup, the inside woven of the warmest and finest possible materials like grass rootlets, lichens, and bits of bark bound together with spider webs. The outside is very carefully covered in bits of fungus or moss to blend the nest with the branches which support it.

The Long-Billed Marsh Wren prefers to hide its nest in tall rushes. It is concealed always with the greatest ingenuity and made of plaited reeds in the shape of a ball. An opening in the side leads to an incubation chamber which is lined with fine materials and is safe against the heaviest rain. The Wren is a tireless builder, for it is not content with just one nest but will build several before its mate chooses the one she will live in.

Birds are very inventive users of materials. The Swallow mixes mud in a puddle in the road, then flies quickly back to its nest with some of it in its beak. When it dries, this mud hardens and forms an attractive cup, thanks to the Swallow's skill. Before laying its eggs, the Swallow lines this cup with grass and down.

Other more wary birds prefer to nest in holes. The Woodpecker busily hollows out a tree trunk, using its strong beak as a drill. When it has made a hole big enough to hold the eggs, it lays them there on a bed of wood shavings.

Woodpeckers are true craftsmen but some birds prefer to use already finished sites, taking advantage of another's work. Among these are Starlings, which often chase the first owners of the nest away.

Great Crested Grebe at home

Great Reed Warbler building a nest

Hairy Woodpecker feeding its young

Tropical Nests

Cave Swiftlet nesting

THERE is a story of the Chinese Emperor Hui Tsung, who came to the throne in the twelfth century at the age of nineteen. One day he attended a meeting of the Academy of Painting where the academicians were returning works to the pupils who had submitted them to the Academy for criticism. The Emperor, wishing to honor a few of the artists whose talents he admired, invited them to dine with him in the Imperial Palace, where the artists were served a delicately scented soup in the finest of porcelain bowls.

The Emperor's soup was made from Swallows' nests and had been for centuries the favorite food of the Court of Peking where it fetched fabulous prices. It would seem to us repulsive to eat nests, for we imagine the nests of our own Swallows, made of mud and straw. The nests so popular in China are built by the Cave Swiftlet, a close relative of our Swift, and are in fact made of a very extraordinary material.

These fast-flying birds live beside the sea and nest in caves whose mouths are washed by the waves. The nests are little white cups about two and a half to three and one quarter inches long and are made entirely of solidified saliva. Swiftlets have enormous salivary glands and secrete a mucus which solidifies as soon as it reaches the air. What could be stranger than an animal that builds a home for its children with secretions from its own body?

These nests were collected by the Chinese at the risk of human life, for huge, vertical rocks had to be scaled. However, the brave climber was rewarded, for the delicacy fetched large sums of money from food-lovers, and the fashion still persists.

The Ovenbird of Brazil builds a sphere-shaped nest of clay. There is a hole on the side which leads into an incubation chamber. The inside of the Ovenbird's clay nest is as smooth as its outside.

The Tailorbirds of Algeria make the outside wall of their nests with leaves which they sew together as skillfully and neatly as would an expert seamstress.

A colony of Sociable Weaverbirds

Weaver at work

their vast nests, which shelter a whole colony and are sometimes in use for one hundred years, convert the tree they choose into a mass of branches, twigs, and threads. Each nest opens below and belongs to a single pair of birds. As many as three hundred separate nests are found together in one dome-shaped structure. The Sociable Weaverbirds deserve their name, and their dwellings make us think of a modern housing development where space is limited and yet each family has its separate dwelling. Weaverbirds adapt well to captivity and many species such as the Java Sparrow, Strawberry Finch and Waxbill are kept as cage pets. Two kinds of Weaverbird that have migrated to the United States are the English or House Sparrow and the European Tree Sparrow.

Other tropical birds are also skilled craftsmen and intersperse threads in the fabric of their nests. No birds are better at this than the Weaverbirds, which are so called because of their great skill at the art of weaving. When building its nest the South African olive and yellow Weaverbird begins by collecting vegetable fibers, often those of the banana tree. Then after shredding the large leaves it takes hold of a fiber in its beak and drops with all its weight so as to tear free a long thread. This it carries to a spot it has chosen, a palm tree or acacia, and knots the lash skillfully around a branch, using its beak and feet. Bit by bit it weaves the threads and finally turns the construction into a fine piece of weaving, resembling the texture of a basket. The result is a good-sized nest in the shape of a bottle. A long entrance hall leads to the downy incubation chamber. The young birds are sheltered from tropical rain and are out of reach of tree snakes, their most dangerous enemies. The snakes cannot enter the nest, since it swings at the end of a flexible branch with the long entrance hall opening toward the ground. As Weaverbirds nest in groups, their chosen trees bear many nests, around which swarm masses of these yellow birds.

Their relatives, the Sociable Weaverbirds, live in even bigger groups. Is it the lack of suitable nesting sites or an extremely sociable instinct which makes them build communal dwellings? We cannot say, but

Tailorbird building its nest

69

Underground Nests

THE Swallows which so often visit our houses and build their nests there are perfect masons, but other Swallows are tunnelers, too.

To discover this, one might follow the course of a river.

The flat bank gives way to a steep one where the river makes a sharp bend. The water has undermined the ground and formed a large shifting bank of sand or clay. Here masses of Bank Swallows with dark plumage on their backs, white necks and bellies, and blackish bands on their chests, are circling. To make their nests these Swallows burrow in the earth of the cliffs, which soon look like a piece of Swiss cheese. The bird grips the wall with its hooked feet and begins to dig with its beak. When it has started a tunnel, its partner comes to relieve it. In a few days, unless a rock or root gets in the way, the birds will have completed a corridor about two inches in diameter and a yard or more deep. At the end of this passage is a spacious room which the Swallows fill with twigs,

wool, and feathers. Here the young will be kept warm and sheltered from the rain. Nest robbers such as snakes and small carnivores are unable to get into this nest.

Unless the winter floods have swept away large pieces of the cliff while the birds were away in Central and South America, Bank Swallows use the same site several times, repairing in the spring the nest which they abandoned the previous autumn.

How Megapodes Hatch

THE modern poultry farmer uses an artificial incubator. In this apparatus, which can be regulated at will, the eggs are assured ideal conditions of humidity and temperature, enabling the chicks to hatch more regularly than those from eggs subjected to the whims of a hen.

Nature developed the incubator long before men did. The woodlands of Australia and New Guinea are inhabited by near relations of the domestic chicken. Having long feet tipped with strong claws, these birds are the size of a cock and are called Megapodes or Mound Birds. The parents, who seem rather careless of their young, build mounds of dead leaves, moss, and humus about ten feet high and forty feet across. Deep inside this mound they bury their eggs, making use of the special kind of humidity in these artificial incubators. The heat given out by the decaying material can reach 100º F. and is more constant than that of the most devoted of mothers. However, the parents keep watch over the mound, for the temperature must not pass a certain level. As soon as the limit is reached, the father opens the mound with his sturdy feet to cool off the inside of this strange construction. When the eggs hatch, the baby Mound Birds make their way out by carving a passage with their strong claws. They do not need the assistance of their parents to introduce them to life.

Megapode hatching its eggs

The Hornbill

Hornbill feeding its young

WE would think the huge-beaked Hornbill a jealous husband from the way he builds his nest. He looks for a large cavity in an old tree in the African or Asian bush. When he has found one the right size, which is not easy since many Hornbills are bigger than a large Crow, his mate gets inside it. The Hornbill then walls up the entrance with mud, leaving only a narrow slit through which the female could not possibly leave. Through this slit the male feeds his mate who is busy hatching her eggs and later caring for her offspring. The incubation chamber is completely closed except for this narrow communication with the outside world. The wall is not broken down until the brood is ready to fly.

There are all sorts of legends about this curious nesting habit. However, the real reason for such a peculiar construction is safety. Enemies, such as snakes and other flesh eaters, cannot get in through the tiny slit.

71

The Cowbird and the Cuckoo

Cowbird

European Cuckoo

THE Cowbird, distant cousin of the Grackle, probably came long ago from tropical America and has spread northward across Mexico to the great plains. As the forests were cleared, the Cowbird gradually penetrated farther east and west, and now it can be seen in gardens and orchards over most of the continent.

These birds used to follow the great herds of bison and now follow domestic cattle. Cowbirds eat insects and catch those which the bison or cows disturb as they move about among the grass and shrubs. Sometimes they pass between the animals' feet and even perch on their backs without in the least annoying the large creatures which they in turn warn of approaching danger.

However, the Cowbird is a dangerous rogue and a shameless parasite of smaller birds. The mother Cowbird shows not the slightest interest in its young and forces smaller birds to bring them up. Although its relatives, the Grackles and Orioles, build very comfortable nests, the Cowbird does not gather together the smallest pile of twigs, so it is not surprising that it never settles down to family life. The female looks over the nests of small birds, particularly those of the Red-Eyed Vireos, Redstarts, Yellow Warblers, Song Sparrows, and Flycatchers. As soon as she has found a nest containing freshly laid eggs, she quickly lays her own egg there, taking advantage of the momentary absence of the nest's rightful owner. She must work quickly, for if the owner discovers the trick it will most likely abandon the nest and build another.

Although the Cowbird's egg is bigger than those of the adoptive parents, they will sit on it as if it were one of their own. As the Cowbird's incubation period is shorter by at least a day, the young Cowbird hatches before its adopted brothers and at once starts demanding food. The adoptive parents bring this greedy bird whatever it wants and it grows very fast. The smaller fledglings are soon pushed aside by their stronger stepbrother. Many Cowbirds have been responsible for the death of an entire brood of Sparrows. Moreover, it is strange to see the large young Cowbird still receiving beakfuls of food from its much smaller adoptive parents.

The Cowbird makes use of the nests of no fewer than eleven kinds of Flycatchers, sixty-two varieties of Sparrows, nine kinds of Vireos, and thirty-six kinds of Warblers.

The European Cuckoo is even more selfish than the American Cowbird. Unlike our Cuckoos, which build their own nests and bring up their own young, the European Cuckoo has lost all trace of family feeling and leaves its eggs to the care of other birds, just

1. A Robin's nest
2. The Cuckoo lays an egg in the Robin's nest and flies away
3. The young Cuckoo hatches
4. It throws the other eggs from the nest
5. Alone in the nest, it demands its food
6. The mother Robin feeds the young Cuckoo

Young Cuckoo fed by a European Robin

Cuckoo egg in a Robin's nest

like the Cowbird. Usually it chooses the nests of Wrens, Reed Warblers, and Wagtails, and the female will lay one egg in each nest, taking care not to be seen. Birds know that the Cuckoo threatens their children's future and will chase it off if they see it.

The Cuckoo's egg is very similar to those of its unsuspecting hosts, so that the trick goes unnoticed. Here again the young Cuckoo hatches twenty-four hours before the rightful heirs. Although blind and naked, it will not rest until it has thrown all the unhatched eggs of the adoptive parents out of the nest.

Once it is alone, it gobbles up everything the parents bring it and grows quickly, soon becoming bigger than its feeders. The latter seem not at all surprised by this and lovingly continue to tend the chick which killed their own children. Thus every European Cuckoo is responsible for the death of a whole brood of baby birds, while the Cowbird often gets on quite well with its adopted brothers, as long as it is well fed.

Birds have a very well-developed family feeling as a rule, but Cuckoos and Cowbirds are exceptions.

Penguins

I T would seem that no animal could live in such a doleful place as Antarctica, where icy winds sweep over the snowy wastes. But behind a cliff of ice we may suddenly discover a colony of Penguins.

There are several species of this strange kind of bird, whose wings are replaced by paddles which enable it to swim with the ease of a fish. On land Penguins look like little men and waddle about in their evening dress and fine starched shirt fronts. This human appearance is accentuated by the fact that Penguins always stand about in groups and seem to be holding conversations.

The Penguin was named such by Spanish navigators in the seventeenth century, because of the great amount of fat beneath the skin. The name Penguin in Spanish means grease.

Although Penguins belong primarily to the Southern Hemisphere, not all of them live in Antarctica. One kind has come as far north as the Galapagos Islands on the equator off the coast of Ecuador. Others, like the Rockhopper Penguins, prefer rocky islands in temperate climates. Rockhoppers are two feet high, and their heads are decorated with orange tufts.

The most impressive of all are the Emperor Penguins, which are over three feet tall and weigh up to eighty-eight pounds. These Penguins are richly dressed in feathers tightly pressed together and as warm as a fur coat. We can recognize them at once by their large size and the black and yellow markings on their heads. They live in colonies of several hundreds and even several thousands, often on ice floes in the ocean.

These birds live in the worst imaginable conditions. The temperature often falls as low as minus forty degrees Fahrenheit and the wind reaches a speed of sixty miles per hour, driving snow and ice before it. The Penguins crowd together into a compact mass with their backs to the wind, to protect themselves as best they can.

When the wind dies down they shake themselves free of the snow which has covered them. Then they form long lines to go fishing on the edge of the ice floe. They walk slowly and solemnly in the manner of people whose legs are too short. When surprised, they lie on their bellies and slide quickly through the snow, propelling themselves with their feet and paddling with their small "wings." They can go as fast as ten miles per hour with this "tobogganing" method on the snow.

The water is their element. They swim with ease and leap out of the water like dolphins. They catch fish, squids, and crustaceans by the pound and can swallow a six-inch-long fish.

To court his future mate the Emperor Penguin offers a pebble to a female. If she picks up the pebble, she has accepted him and they mate. Unlike other birds, the Emperor Penguin lays its single egg at the beginning of winter, when the polar night falls on this uninhabited continent. It would be extremely difficult to build a nest where there is nothing but ice

Emperor Penguins

and snow, so the Emperor Penguin prefers to place its egg on its feet and then cover it with an ample fold of its lower abdomen, thus forming a pocket where the egg will be kept nice and warm. The bird still manages to walk with little steps, keeping the egg on its feet. This method of incubation is communal. The incubating egg is passed from one Penguin to another so that each of them can go fishing and stretch its legs.

In August, while we are strolling on sunny beaches, the young birds hatch in the middle of the polar winter. No young bird is prettier than the Penguin chick, dressed in silvery gray except for the black and white markings on its head. At first the chicks shelter in the incubating pockets of the adults, who fight violently over them. The poor little fledglings are sometimes badly hurt through the excessive attention of the adults. Later the young birds are gathered into nursery schools just like children. There, under the supervision of a few adults, they await the return of the fishermen-Penguins who will bring them freshly caught fish. When the terrible blizzards come, Penguins encircle their young and, their backs bent against the wind, form an "insulated wall" to protect the next Penguin generations.

The recent explorations of man in Antarctica have led to a reduction of the numbers of the colonies of Penguins. Their gregarious nesting habits and poor locomotion on land make them easy prey for man who hunts both the eggs and birds for food.

Ostriches

THE Ostrich is sometimes called the Camel Bird. Like the camel, it lives on dry and sometimes desertlike grasslands, in Africa and the Near East. It makes up for its lack of useful wings with its well-developed legs and feet. Like the Camel, it has only two toes, and this makes it unique among birds. This foot construction enables it to run extremely fast on hard, dry ground.

What silly things people say about this tall and powerful bird! One completely unfounded legend is that when pursued by enemies the Ostrich hides its head in the sand, thinking that as it can no longer see, it cannot be seen.

It is true that the Ostrich will swallow any bright object within reach of its beak. A traveler tells that an Ostrich once swallowed a candlestick he had left lying around near the cage of one of these birds destined for the zoo. The object in question, too big to enter the bird's digestive tract, was finally brought up, whole but fantastically twisted by its gizzard muscles. Other Ostriches have swallowed as much as eleven pounds of metal, nails, chains and even pieces of pottery and china.

The male Ostrich has magnificent, white silky wing feathers. He uses these feathers to win his mate in a courting display, in which he dances and contorts himself. He collects a harem of about four or five females, often won in tough fights with his rivals. These wives lay eggs in a communal nest, if it can be so called, for it is nothing but a dip in the ground where the eggs are laid side by side, sometimes as many as thirty together. Each egg measures about six and a half by five inches.

The male bird takes care of the hatching, only occasionally being relieved by his wives. At midday when the sun has warmed the air sufficiently, there is no need to continue sitting on the eggs, and they are left alone, with a light covering of sand. These splendid eggs are a tempting prey, particularly for jackals, which gobble them up. Tradition has it that the eggs in the middle of the "nest" are surrounded by unfertilized eggs which could never produce a young Ostrich, so that their loss has no effect on the brood.

One Ostrich egg is equivalent to about twenty Hens' eggs and forty minutes are required to hard boil an Ostrich egg. A single Ostrich egg could make an eggnog which would serve about fifty people.

After about six weeks the young Ostriches hatch. Each weighs about two pounds and is covered with a very special plumage which makes it look like a hedgehog perched on long legs. It is a full-time job for the father to control these busy young things who are ready to leave and hunt for seeds, berries, and insects.

He must also protect his family from enemies and he does this very bravely. When a flock of running Ostriches is on the point of being caught, the male bird bringing up the rear attempts a diversion. He suddenly changes direction and falls as if injured. He gets up heavily and then falls again. This attracts the attention of the pursuers, happy that they can thus so easily capture the best bird of the flock. But

A group of Ostriches in Africa

as soon as the females and the young are safely away, the male Ostrich gets up and flees with huge strides, often leaving his pursuers panting and completely fooled by a bird reputed to be stupid. His speed may reach fifty miles per hour for a distance of one half mile.

By the end of their first year the Ostriches gain their adult weight, approximately 220 pounds, which makes these birds the biggest in the world at the present time.

Raising the Fledglings

WHEN the fledglings are hatched, the hardest work of the year begins for parent birds. Their starving offspring demand food from morning to night, so the parents have to hunt incessantly and are forever coming and going to feed their fledglings with insects and small worms. Chickadees return to the nest nearly four hundred times a day with mouthfuls of food for their large family of as many as six to eight young birds. They have been seen coming to the nest eighty times in an hour.

Young birds of prey are also unable to leave the nest. Their parents bring food which they have caught for them. Their mother dismembers the prey and feeds it to them bit by bit and they swallow it greedily.

Some birds, such as the chicks of the domestic Hen, are covered in down on hatching. They can walk a few hours after birth, so they leave the nest very early and follow their parents who at once begin to teach them. At the slightest danger, they answer their mother's call and hide under her wings. They also spend the night or wait for the rain to stop in this downy shelter.

Some birds, Pigeons, for example, are naked and weak when they hatch. They cannot leave their nest, and the parents must continue sitting on the nest to keep them warm. For the first few days of their lives, young Pigeons feed on a milky substance secreted in the parents' crops.

After a certain time, about two or three weeks with small birds, the young are ready to fly. They seem very afraid to leave the nest or jump into the air in spite of the encouragement of their parents. When they do learn to fly, the family still stays together, even if only to allow the parents to continue to feed the young birds, neatly lined up on a branch. Bit by bit the fledglings gain confidence. Soon they are as experienced as their parents. They go off on their own, often leaving the place where they were born.

A new generation of birds is ready to enchant our woods and valleys.

Mallard duck and ducklings

MIGRATION

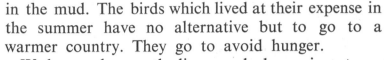

FOR many people an ideal life would be to spend spring in town, summer by the sea or in the mountains, and winter in a warm country. Many of our birds have made this dream a reality. Every year migrants undertake very long journeys; many of our summer visitors could not live if they did not travel. What food could Swifts and Swallows find in the cold winter air, and Warblers in the leafless trees? The insects by then have disappeared, their nymphs and larvae buried deep in their hiding places in tree trunks or the ground. In the Far North how could ducks and shore birds live on frozen lakes hidden under a thick coat of snow? Frogs are hibernating and mollusks are deeply buried

in the mud. The birds which lived at their expense in the summer have no alternative but to go to a warmer country. They go to avoid hunger.

We have only recently discovered where migrants go. For a long time it was assumed that birds went to sleep in the autumn like cold-blooded animals. It was thought that Swallows gathered among the rushes and plunged into the water where they spent the winter. This belief was still held by the famous scholar Linnaeus at the end of the eighteenth century. Whimsical writers imagined that birds left our countries to spend the winter on the moon.

Fanciful theories have been replaced by a deeper knowledge of bird migrations. We now know where migratory birds spend the winter, and how they travel, but there remain many mysteries to be solved. The most exciting concerns the birds' sense of direction, an extremely important phenomenon which still needs clarification. We sometimes get lost in the town where we live, or wander off course on a walk in the country, but the little Swallow, which leaves our roof-tops in autumn and goes to the Amazon basin or the Argentine, is able to find its nesting place again the following spring without making a mistake, having traveled as much as six thousand miles. It is as if birds carry a compass which leads them steadfastly to their destination following the earth's magnetic field. But the explanation is not a simple one. No one knows just why birds migrate, but reasons of heredity, instinct, secretions of glands, and responses to light may be influential. Food supply seems to be very important, more so than temperature. Birds leave colder areas and fly south to find food in winter, then again fly north in summer to escape competition. Some birds migrate by day, but most migrate by night. The migrations north and south are the best known. Some birds move only a few hundred miles from their breeding to their winter range while others cover several thousand miles. The champion migrating bird is probably the Plover, who travels nonstop the 2,400 miles between Alaska and Hawaii.

79

Banding a Mallard
that has been trapped

Banding of Birds

Bands from various
countries in the world

How a bird should
be held for banding

A T the beginning of this century a young Dane, intrigued by the journeys of the Storks which nested near his house, attached a medallion bearing his name and address to the leg of one of these wading birds. The following year the Stork returned bearing a little object from Benares, the holy city in India. This exchange of messages continued the next year and resulted in the marriage of the young Dane and the daughter of an English settler of Benares, who had met through this migratory bird.

The happy ending is probably fictional, but this anecdote illustrates many of the experiments which have been going on for a long time in the study of the movements of birds. Pliny, the Roman naturalist, reported that in the first century A.D. a Roman who was enthusiastic about chariot racing brought Swallows with him to the races where he freed them, having dyed their feathers the color of the winning team. This was to inform his friends in the country of the winners.

It was not until the beginning of the twentieth century that ornithologists began to use truly scientific methods. Now a band is fixed around the leg of the migrant in the form of an aluminum bracelet bearing the abbreviated address of the institution in charge of these operations, and a number. This band is to the bird like the identity card of a citizen or the serial number of a soldier. It enables one to find the name of the bird by referring to the banding card index, as well as the place where it was banded and the date. When the bird is found, either killed by a hunter or by accident, or captured by a bird-watching station, its route can be estimated.

Thanks to these bands, a Guatemalan hunting in the forest of Peten is able to tell that the Duck he has just killed was migrating from the marshes of Saskatchewan or Dakota, where it was hatched, to spend the winter beside the great rivers of South America. An Arctic Tern banded in New Brunswick, Canada, was identified by its band while spending

Wild Geese flying in V formation

the winter at the Cape in South Africa, and another banded at the same time was found at La Rochelle in France.

The bands which we place on our birds carry a serial number and the words: "Write Fish and Wildlife Service, Washington D. C., U.S.A."

How are birds banded? First you must obtain the necessary permission to make a suitable trap in your garden. Then you must catch the birds you want to mark and even more important have the specialized knowledge to recognize them perfectly, for it is essential to note exactly the kind of birds you are to band. The person who finds them may not be an ornithologist, but more probably a hunter, a fisherman, or a farmer.

To catch as many birds as possible, bird-watching stations have been set up on the most important migratory routes on which large numbers of birds travel. Usually the number of banded birds recovered is very small. Ducks are most frequently found because they are hunted, but no more than twenty per cent of wild fowl banded are recovered. Among little birds the proportion is even smaller. Of 16,203 Warblers

banded at a single time, only fifteen were recaptured. So tens of thousands of birds must be banded to plot the migratory routes of our commonest birds.

Every year bird-watching stations band a large number of migrants. Since its foundation, the American banding organization, now dependent on the Fish and Wildlife Service, has placed more than 11 million bands on the legs of birds of six hundred different species. Each year 600,000 birds are banded. The organization has been advised of 900,000 recaptured birds so far, and up to forty or fifty thousand are added yearly to this enormous list which enables us to follow the migrants on their lengthy travels.

The small proportion of recoveries makes it the duty of each one of us to send back bands we may discover as soon as possible, as well as all the information about how and where we found them. Do not follow the example of the fisherman who kept bands as souvenirs in his tobacco pouch, or some African natives who keep them as beads on a necklace. We can all become helpers in a research project which exists for the better protection of birds and which has laboratories covering the whole world.

Where Do North American Birds Go?

Bobolink

A T the end of August, autumn begins to turn the leaves brown. This is the time for the Bobolink to contemplate its yearly journey. It has stopped singing its characteristic song, which consists of joyfully vibrant metallic notes and is one of the most beautiful sounds in North America. The young birds, sheltered in the summer in nests hidden on the ground among the long grasses, are now grown and are ready to desert their native land, which will soon become inhospitable.

The Bobolinks leave their summer quarters and go southward. After lingering in the Gulf states, they cross the Gulf of Mexico, calling at Cuba and Jamaica, and arrive at last in Northern Colombia and Venezuela. Bobolinks seem to be particularly fearless, for few of our birds have the courage to cross the sea and prefer to follow the longer route over Central America.

Even when they arrive in South America, the Bobolinks have still not reached the end of their journey. They have to cross the forests of the Amazon and the endless pampas before they come to the marshes of Argentina, which is where these tireless migrants spend the winter.

The Bobolink is only one of the many migratory birds. Some of our less demanding birds converge on parts of the United States that remain warm during the winter. To reach these states, millions of migrants follow the Atlantic coast, passing along the dunes and collecting along the way in privileged places such as Cape May in New Jersey and Cape Charles in Virginia, where thousands of bird watchers come each year to see them pass. Others come down the Mississippi Valley, one of the most important flyways of North America. This great route, interspersed with marshes and resting places, is followed from Alaska and the Northwest Territories of Canada by Ducks and Geese, which spend the winter not far from the Gulf of Mexico. When hastened by the cold, millions of Ducks pass over the central part of the United States in a few days. After having flown at a speed of fifty miles an hour and at heights of fifteen hundred to three thousand feet, half a million Ducks have been known to arrive in Louisiana in a single October. Thousands of bands which had been placed on these birds in their summer quarters or as they had

MIGRATION OF THE BOBOLINK

Nesting areas

- - - - - Migration routes

Winter quarters

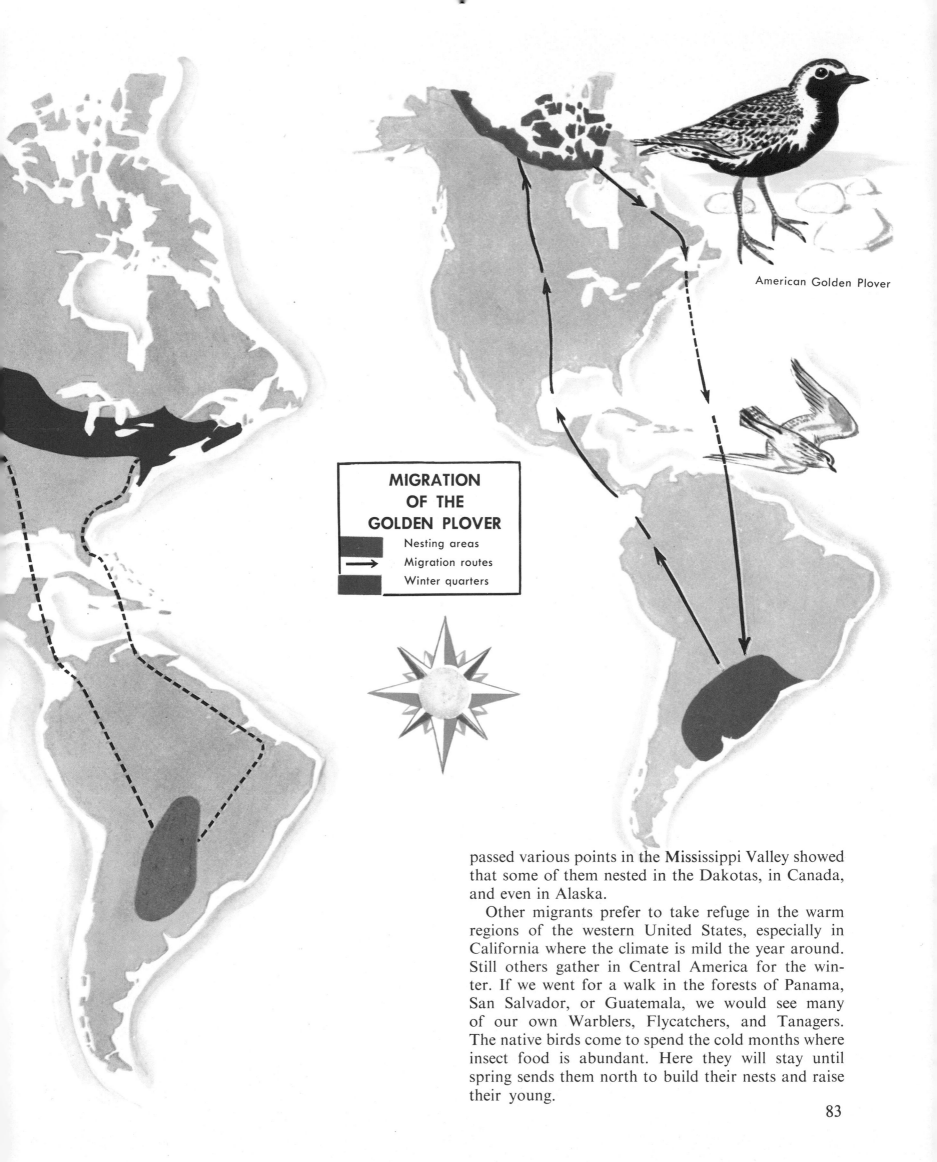

American Golden Plover

MIGRATION OF THE GOLDEN PLOVER
- Nesting areas
- → Migration routes
- Winter quarters

passed various points in the Mississippi Valley showed that some of them nested in the Dakotas, in Canada, and even in Alaska.

Other migrants prefer to take refuge in the warm regions of the western United States, especially in California where the climate is mild the year around. Still others gather in Central America for the winter. If we went for a walk in the forests of Panama, San Salvador, or Guatemala, we would see many of our own Warblers, Flycatchers, and Tanagers. The native birds come to spend the cold months where insect food is abundant. Here they will stay until spring sends them north to build their nests and raise their young.

83

Where Do European Birds Winter?

THE Swallows of Europe gather in flocks on telegraph wires. They wheel in the September sky and disappear, bound for Africa where they spend the winter.

These fast-flying birds meet great dangers, but they are well-suited to such long flights. If they linger in Europe, the Swallows risk being surprised by a sudden cold spell which will kill off their favorite insects and leave them starving. So they set off knowing they must cross the Mediterranean before the storms which are frequent in spring and autumn. After a pause in the greener parts of North Africa, they are confronted with the next obstacle, the Sahara Desert. They rest now and then at an occasional oasis, but vast stretches of sand must be crossed, with not a tree or bush to shelter them from the intense cold of the night and the burning heat of the day. When the greener Sudan is reached, their trials are nearly over, although many Swallows are lost in tropical tornadoes. But they are not satisfied with these very pleasant regions and press on as far as the Cape of Good Hope, as much as 6,200 miles from their native land. What a traveler's tale could be told by the bird that comes back to nest under an English roof in the spring! It could tell of endless desert and luxuriant virgin forest. Before the Swallow returns to perch on the telephone wire, it will have perched on palm trees, on thatched roofs of African straw huts, and on baobab trees, the giants of the equatorial forests, with bulging trunks shaped like bottles.

In the spring it is easy to tell when the migrants have returned, for each bird announces its arrival with characteristic song. However, their fall departure is much quieter. Birds are silent once their young have grown up. But, although they are quiet, their departure is still spectacular, for many assemble beforehand in flocks of thousands.

In Europe the Cuckoo is the first to leave. Always solitary, it goes not in a group but alone. After July its two-syllabled cry can no longer be heard in the woods. It has already left for tropical Africa.

On an August morning the sky is suddenly emptied of Swifts. For some days they have been making less noise and preparing for their journey They, too, seek the sun of tropical Africa for the winter.

The Golden Oriole leaves at the same time, going the roundabout way. It lingers by the Mediterranean when the figs are ripe and then continues to Africa.

Storks gather on the damp plains of Germany during the last days of August. The solemn flocks are inspected by one of their number and then spiral up into the sky to disappear over the horizon, Africa bound. Storks seem to have an inherited sense of direction. If a young Stork is blown off course or becomes lost from the rest of the flock, it will eventually find the way to Africa, a land where it has never been.

In September and October the small birds hurry in countless flocks along the migratory routes, often flying only at night and resting and feeding during the day. If you look at the full moon through binoculars or a low-powered telescope, you will be able to see thousands of birds, many of them too small to be recognized, crossing the light path.

In October squadrons of Cranes flying in V-formation make the air ring with their discordant cries. This is also the best time to observe huge gatherings of migrating shore birds. Thousands of Sandpipers, Plovers, and Curlews are gathered together in preparation for their journey south. Some will go as far as Africa. Others will stay along the European shores of the Mediterranean.

The Arctic Tern, one of the greatest travelers of all birds, breeds in North America and other regions around the North Pole. Crossing first to Europe, it then flies down the West African Coast to its wintering grounds more than eleven thousand miles away.

The European Starling is proof of one theory of migration, substantiated also for a number of other species. This is that birds find their way by a form of sun navigation. These Starlings are known to orient themselves by the position of the sun, and when the sun is obscured are unable to find their sense of direction; they can even be fooled by the reflection of the sun from mirrors.

Not all European birds migrate. Some birds stay behind. While the open country is left to the Crows, others, such as the Tits, Robins, Kinglets, and friendly Wrens come closer to houses as if to promise that spring will come again.

MIGRATION OF THE EUROPEAN STORK

The dark green zones indicate the nesting areas.
The dotted lines show the migration routes.

Geese, Swans, and Ducks

As we have seen, winter scatters our birds, many of which flee to Central and South America. On the other hand, enormous flocks of Ducks arrive in the southeastern states and on the Atlantic coast, coming from Canada, Alaska, and the northern states. Winter has frozen the lakes of their homeland, making it impossible for these birds to satisfy their voracious appetites. The mollusks are deeply embedded in the mud and there are no more insects, worms, water plants, and grain for them to eat.

The journeys of these Ducks are infinitely varied. Many, like the Canvasback, cross the entire North American continent. The male Canvasback has a bright rusty-red head and neck contrasting with its black breast and gray back. The female is grayish, with a reddish tinge on her head. They nest in Alaska and Canada and fly from there in the autumn toward the southeast. After crossing the Great Lakes they press on eastward until they reach the coast, while some of their number fly due south down the Mississippi Valley. Most of them spend the winter on the Atlantic seaboard, especially in Virginia and North Carolina, where they find varied food in the many inlets. However, they do not find here their favorite food—the wild celery buds which they search for in their nesting places. Their completely vegetarian diet—ducks can go as deep as thirty feet under water to look for water plants—must have something to do with their flesh's delicate flavor. They are much sought after by hunters along their migratory routes.

The Geese and Swans of the far north follow the Ducks on their seasonal travels. Canada Geese descend in flocks to the southern states for the winter, flying in squadrons of V-formation. The older male birds lead the squadrons calling the familiar "honk, honk." They are answered by their followers. To reach a safe resting place where they can land in peace, Canada Geese fly night and day without stopping. They are the wariest and most intelligent of all web-footed birds.

Canada Geese are also the most faithful among birds, for a pair will live together all their lives, traveling side by side on their long and dangerous journeys. It is said that when one dies, the other never again mates.

Green-Winged Teal

Shoveler

Tufted Duck

Widgeon

Pochard

Mallard (drake)

Mallard (duck)

Canvasback

Pintail

Golden-Eye

Shelduck

Barnacle Goose

Brent Goose

Whooper Swan

BIRDS' activities vary the year around, but each month brings new pleasures to the bird lover. The rhythm of bird life is particularly interesting in the northeastern states where the seasons are well defined.

In January the Great Horned Owl begins to utter its cry, which echoes through the night as the harbinger of spring. It is a cry easy to recognize for it has two modulated notes, one long and one short.

In February the flocks of Chickadees which fill our gardens begin to return to the woods. Every day their repertoire of songs increases.

With the arrival of spring in March, the Eastern Phoebe, one of our hardiest migrants, returns and starts to hunt the early insects, and as if to announce that it is back it begins making the persistent "Phoebe" call that gave it its name.

By April, migration is in full swing. Birds return north *en masse*, particularly Warblers. This, too, is the season when birds' plumage is at its brightest.

In May and June, the birds build their nests and birdsong is heard everywhere. From morning till night, birds are constantly on the go, and some of them do not even stop at night.

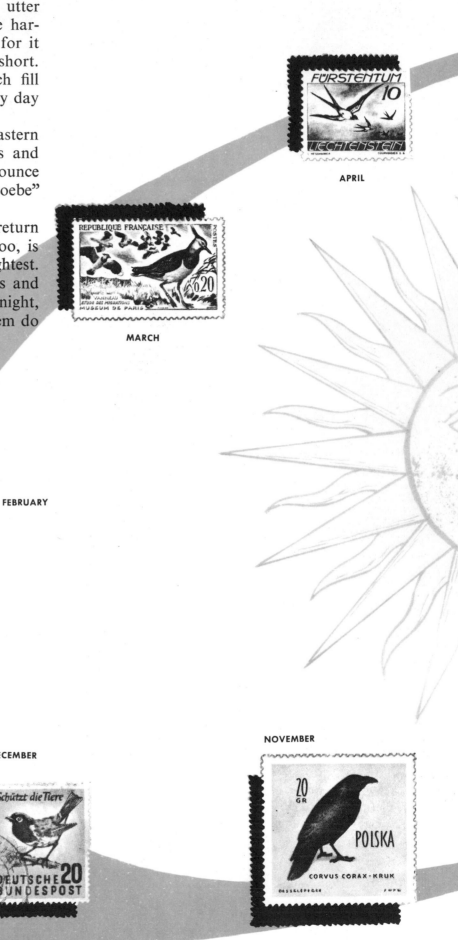

The Bird

APRIL

MARCH

FEBRUARY

JANUARY

DECEMBER

NOVEMBER

Watchers' Year

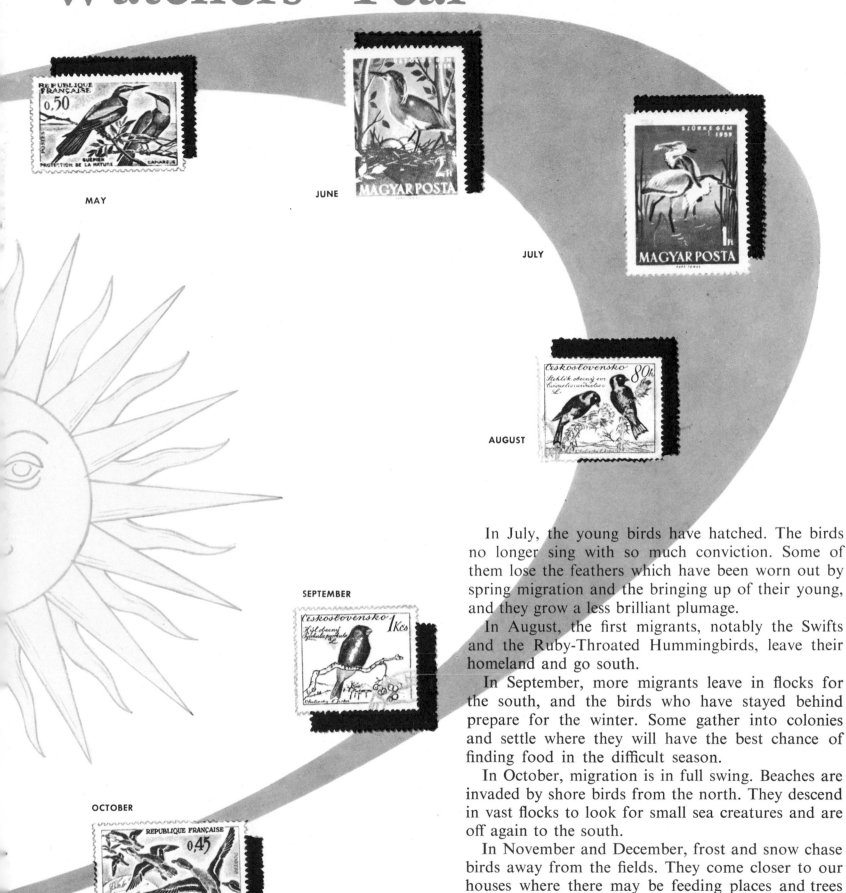

MAY

JUNE

JULY

AUGUST

SEPTEMBER

OCTOBER

In July, the young birds have hatched. The birds no longer sing with so much conviction. Some of them lose the feathers which have been worn out by spring migration and the bringing up of their young, and they grow a less brilliant plumage.

In August, the first migrants, notably the Swifts and the Ruby-Throated Hummingbirds, leave their homeland and go south.

In September, more migrants leave in flocks for the south, and the birds who have stayed behind prepare for the winter. Some gather into colonies and settle where they will have the best chance of finding food in the difficult season.

In October, migration is in full swing. Beaches are invaded by shore birds from the north. They descend in vast flocks to look for small sea creatures and are off again to the south.

In November and December, frost and snow chase birds away from the fields. They come closer to our houses where there may be feeding places and trees whose berries attract birds in winter. We may find Woodpeckers, Chickadees, Nuthatches, as well as Sparrows from the north and the Cardinal whose red coat makes a vivid splash of color in the monotonous winter landscape.

It Is Not Good-Bye

WE could think of the migrants as ungrateful birds. They take advantage of our resources during the summer and as soon as the weather turns cold they leave, while we face the rigors of winter.

Their food supply is sufficient only in the summer, when insects and seeds are numerous. Because they sense this, birds actually start their southern journeys before insects and seeds become scarce. They know that if they remained in their summer homes instead of migrating, nothing would be left for them to eat. So they leave to spend two-thirds of the year "on vacation," away from their real homes after nesting and raising their families.

We must not blame them for going. The migrants must leave us in the winter, for most of them would soon die of cold and hunger.

They visit warm countries rich in insects, fruit, and grain. But probably our migrants are never completely happy there. None of them sing when they are in tropical forests; and they search for a place to live which reminds them of home. Swallows take up their quarters among the rushes and Warblers live in trees and bushes, reserving their serenades for us when they return with the coming of spring. In spite of the abundant food, none of them remain in Africa, or Central and South America.

The increasing day-length after December twenty-first is believed to have an important effect on migrants. It is believed to be contributory to the production of a hormone in birds which enables body fat to be stored for their migration journeys beginning as spring advances.

European Roller

BIRDS AND MAN

WHENEVER a Stone-Age man left his cave, a marvelous sight met his eyes. In the swampy plains all kinds of birds were to be found. Thousands of wild fowl were roaming about with countless little waders. Farther off in the dense forests there were quantities of gallinaceous game birds, which showed little fear at the approach of man. In autumn millions of migrants came from the north and their flocks darkened the sky as they passed.

Since those far-off times, the human population has increased considerably and the earth has been transformed. The marshes have been drained and the forests cut down to provide new fields. As a result of these changes, many of the big woodland birds are gradually disappearing, particularly those which used to live in the great eastern forests of the United States.

We still may see many birds on our nature walks. No official census of birds has ever been made, but it is estimated that there are between five and six billion breeding land birds in this country plus an unknown number of water birds. This number was probably far greater when the settlers came to America.

However, many birds multiply at a great rate. A Thrush raises two broods of four birds every year.

This bird can live for about ten years, so if none of its descendants died and all multiplied at the same rate, the total number of Thrushes descended from the original pair would well exceed 19 million after ten years. Hummingbirds and Nighthawks have two chicks, other small birds four or five, Wrens and Chickadees eight or ten, and some Ducks and Rails as many as fifteen. This overproduction always happens, as there must be a sufficient supply of youngsters growing up to offset the accidents that are destined to occur. Each bird has its own special enemies as well as a special set of dangers that it may encounter.

But no bird has so many descendants. This is because young birds have a high death rate. Only forty per cent of the eggs laid produce young which live to leave the nest. In their first year of life many more die, so that, apart from occasional exceptions, from year to year the bird population does not increase.

Added to losses by natural causes are those for which man is responsible. In the last century the hunter was the big threat to birds. The hunting of birds is a much more widespread activity than most people realize, and game laws were for a long time not very good. Plume hunting and the collecting of nests and eggs have also been responsible for the destruction of billions of birds. Hunters kill so many Pheasants that the amount of Pheasant meat consumed in a single year is equivalent to that of fifty thousand cattle.

A man who kills birds is deprived of numerous benefits. Our feathered friends protect us from many dangers, particularly from insects and rats which would otherwise eat our crops. In every country the beauty and songs of birds are a source of pleasure and enjoyment for those who live near them. You can attract them to your lawn or garden by providing food, water, and shelter. Some birds will come for food tossed on the ground and others only to feeders.

ONE day in 1406 the French Queen Isabeau de Bavière, wife of Charles VI, was feeling very excited in the ancient castle of the Louvre in Paris. She adored animals, especially birds which she kept in expensive aviaries, but on this day she did not have eyes even for her white-feathered Goldfinch in its silver cage. The Queen had heard about some wonderful songbirds which a French nobleman was going to bring her from the Canary Islands.

The nobleman returned to the court with the most marvelous songsters that had hitherto been heard in France, the Canaries. The French called them "Serins" after the sirens in Greek legends, the mermaids who lured sailors onto rocks with their beautiful songs.

Cage Birds

For a long time Canaries remained luxuries reserved for kings and princes, as they were rare and quite expensive. King Louis XI of France favored them and bought 330 on one occasion in 1480. A century later the great explorer Sir Walter Raleigh brought some Canaries as a present for Queen Elizabeth I of England. At first she was disappointed at their dull

Euphonia

Canary

Pin-Tailed Widow Bird

Common Waxbill

Cardinal

Red-Throated Parrot-Finch

Gouldian Finch

Superb Tanager

Java Sparrow

Red-Headed Quelea

Red-Cheeked Cordon-Bleu

grayish color, for she had expected them to be as gaily dressed as birds she had received previously. But when after a few days they began to sing beautifully, they so charmed the Queen that she made them her daily companions. They soon began to multiply in the royal aviaries. One day, one of the fledglings began to moult and found itself clothed in golden yellow feathers. The event was considered a miracle and even Shakespeare makes mention of it in his writings.

Since then, Canaries have spread everywhere and almost everyone can afford to buy one. The beauty of this bird's feathers and the quality of its voice have been vastly improved by careful breeding. In comparing the song of the Harz Canary, which can sing runs, trills, and fluting notes, to that of the Cini Canary, its wild cousin living in the countryside of Europe, one finds as vast a difference as between a

and Pets

Blue and Yellow Macaw

Budgerigar

talented opera singer and an untrained voice. The Canary is considered the hardiest of cage birds and is naturally clean in habit.

Among other cage birds are Parakeets and Parrots, the latter distinguished from the former by shorter tails and bulkier appearance. Parakeets were brought to Greece from India in 330 B.C. by the soldiers of Alexander the Great. They made a sensation, and the Romans later paid huge sums of gold for them.

It was not until 1840 that the great naturalist Gould introduced the commonest Parakeet to Europe. This was the Budgerigar which arrived in enormous shipments, as many as 100,000 birds at a time. Budgerigars possess a remarkable ability of imitating human speech. Birds with vocabularies of more than one hundred words have been reported.

In the Middle Ages, Parrots were very popular in Europe. Their popularity was increased by the discovery of new species by travelers. The first bird whose gift for speaking had been noticed was the African Gray Parrot, gray in color with a red tail. In 1500 a Cardinal paid one hundred gold *ecus* in Rome for one of these birds. Later, Macaws were introduced from America, where the Indians exchanged these gaudy birds for glass trinkets. Later still, when mer-

chants sailed to Malaya for precious spices and to the islands around Australia, they brought back magnificent Parrots, such as the brilliantly colored Lories. New kinds were continually being discovered, each more beautiful than the last. King Louis XIV of France commissioned his naval captains to buy Parrots at every port of call, so he could present them to his courtiers.

Parrots are still much sought after for their rich colors and their gaiety. They are also popular for their gift as talkers which varies according to species and according to individual birds. The most gifted birds can remember whole sentences which they repeat, sometimes at inappropriate moments.

Our most familiar and usual pets are the green-bodied Parrots, with various head and tail markings of yellow and blue feathers. They are found in their natural habitat from Mexico through Panama, and along the Amazon River.

Parrots live to a great age and some have become historic. In May of 1929 one died in England which had belonged to Maréchal Masséna, a friend of Napoleon. It was the only creature still living at that time said to have spoken with the Emperor, who died in 1821.

93

Domestic Fowl

CAVEMEN were foremost huntsmen. They sharpened and polished flints to make spear and arrowheads. Birds provided great delicacies for them, particularly when great flocks of migrants were passing by.

They were able to catch some of the birds alive. They put these live birds in enclosures to keep until they had a poor hunting day. These captives laid eggs, which were considered good eating. Later, probably, a clutch went unnoticed in the shadow near a prehistoric farmyard. Soon chicks hatched from these eggs to the delight of the cavemen who had just discovered how to domesticate animals. It didn't take man long to appreciate the value of poultry, once he had caught his first wild fowl and found its eggs and meat delicious.

The first domesticated fowl was the Chicken. This gallinaceous bird came from the warm countries of Asia where it still lives in the wild state. Man brought it with him across Persia and Egypt into Europe. It appeared in Greece in the sixth century B.C., and later in Rome, and in Gaul. The Cock was often thought of as sacred by the Gauls, who made it their emblem, and by the Romans, whose soothsayers considered it could foretell the future.

Since those distant times we have transformed the characteristics of the once wild birds by careful breeding. The colorful fowls in our farmyards would have been unable to survive in the wilderness of their predecessors, but they give twenty times as many eggs as their ancestors, and their flesh is tender and delicious.

Ducks and Geese were domesticated by the ancient Egyptians. There are wall paintings in Egyptian tombs representing each stage in the breeding of web-footed birds. They were kept in fields and gorged with food very scientifically before being taken to special markets. Domesticated Ducks are not as far removed from their wild state as are Chickens. They can still fly well and occasionally one will escape to fly after a female Wild Duck and start a family with her among the rushes of a pond.

Domestic Geese were much favored by the Romans whom they once saved from a catastrophe. In 390 B.C., the Gauls had overrun Italy under their chief, Brennus, and the Romans were forced to retreat to the fortress on the Capitoline Hill, which was their only refuge after losing many battles. The Gauls laid siege to this last bastion. They took advantage of a dark

Turkey

night to make a silent advance on the fortress, but they did not take into consideration a flock of sacred Geese. By honking, these birds gave the alarm, warning the Romans who had time to gather their arms and repel the attack. In recognition of this, the Romans held a procession every year in which a Goose richly dressed in gold was led through the city.

The common Domestic Goose is highly prized for its flesh, eggs, and soft feathers. Although it has been domesticated for a very long time it shows only slight variation from its ancestors, being generally lighter in plumage and bigger in size. Two common breeds of Domestic Geese are the Embden and Toulouse. As its flesh is the tastier of the two, the

Domesticated
Jungle Fowl

Rouen Duck

Goose

Guinea-Fowl

Muscovy Duck

white Embden is preferred for the table, but the gray Toulouse is the better breeder and more numerous. The Chinese Goose is another variety of Domestic Goose that has been bred in Europe and America, and makes delicious eating. African Geese mature early and are favored by farmers since they are marketable within ten weeks.

Guinea Fowl came from Africa where their wild relatives still inhabit the bush, but it was not until the discovery of America that man tasted the Barbary Duck. In spite of its name, this bird does not come from North Africa but from Peru, where it had long been domesticated by the Indians. The domestic Turkey is the only race of poultry that has come from wild stocks native to America. Not only was the meat of Turkey relished by the native Indians, but they also used its feathers to decorate headgear and to make robes and blankets. The Turkey still has wild relatives living in the forests of the United States and in Mexico. It made a notable appearance in Europe and was considered a royal dish. It went to Europe in time to replace Herons and Peacocks which were served in the Middle Ages on special occasions. These days, people do not eat Peacocks, one of the most beautiful ornaments in our parks. As for the Heron, its fishy taste makes it unpleasant to our palates, which are accustomed to the succulent fowl we raise.

Guano Birds

Guanay

CORMORANTS, Boobies, and Pelicans, which live in flocks of about 15 million birds on islands in the Pacific along the coast of Peru, eat a quantity of fish estimated at five million tons every year. In the same length of time fishermen along the coast bring in only four thousand tons in their nets. These strange-looking birds far surpass man in fishing ability.

These sea birds are the world's most concentrated single source of fertilizers. Agriculture makes use of the guano which comes from their droppings to fertilize sugar cane and cotton plants as well as other crops.

The Pacific islands where these bird colonies are established are small and deserted. Nothing grows there and rain never falls. Yet the bird population is incredibly heavy. To approach a colony of over a million Bougainville Cormorants, or Guanayes, the commonest of these birds, is to hear a sound like that of a distant squadron of airplanes. In the mating season the density of population is twelve birds to the square yard, a record unequaled anywhere else in the world. The nests consist of a few stones put together, for there are no other nesting materials available. There is an average of three nests to the square yard, with six adults and six young, each couple bringing up at least two chicks. It is difficult for the parents to find their offspring in this crowd, but each bird recognizes its nest, its mate, and its children. The slightest mistake can set off a riot.

The fish which these birds live on are abundant. They are brought by the current from the seas of Antarctica to the equator. Little anchovies are especially favored by the birds. It has been estimated that there must be 10,000 billion of them in the waters around these Pacific islands, making a total of twenty million tons.

The droppings of these masses of birds accumulate on the islands. Their resting places look as if they were covered by snow. This deposit is never washed away by rain and is allowed to accumulate over several years. Then it is collected with shovels and pickaxes,

Variegated Piquero

GUANO ISLANDS

PERU

SOUTH AMERICA

Collecting guano

loaded into ships, exported, pulverized, and spread on the fields as fertilizer.

This process has been going on for centuries. The Inca kings, whose empire flourished from the tenth century until the time of the Spanish conquest in 1531, organized the collection of guano. Modern Peru goes to great length to preserve this unusual and profitable natural resource.

The high value of guano is due to the fact that it is a general fertilizer, yielding all the ingredients of plant food in a condition that can be readily assimilated.

Since it can be trained to hunt in captivity, the Bougainville Cormorant has sometimes been called "the world's most useful bird." This bird is also very skilled in obtaining its prey. It feeds exclusively on fish, diving from the surface of the water, seizing its prey, tossing it in the air and efficiently recatching it so that it may be more easily swallowed. Fishermen in China and Japan have used this bird's services since ancient times.

Falconry

Falcon at rest on its master's hand

FALCONS sweep down on plains from high in the air to seize unsuspecting birds and carry their prey off with admirable grace and skill. This gave man the idea of using the services of these birds to hunt feathered game. It was in this way that falconry was born. The Greeks and Romans practiced the sport, which was also very fashionable in the Middle Ages. Knights returning from the Crusades in the Middle East were able to perfect their technique after watching Oriental falconers, who were particularly skilled in the breeding and training of birds of prey.

Much patience is needed to train a Falcon or an Eagle to hunt for man's benefit. The bird must first learn to remain quietly on the hunter's wrist, which is protected with a leather glove. Then the falconer trains the bird to take the bait, a piece of the skin of its future prey. When the bird has learned to return obediently to the wrist, it is used to capture various birds such as Pigeons, Quails, and Magpies.

Inhabitants of the central Asian steppes hunt foxes, wolves, roe deer, and gazelles, using specially trained Eagles. They follow their prey on horseback with the Eagle sitting on a special saddle. At the right moment they let the bird fly and it kills the animal with its claws and strong bill.

Carrier Pigeons

SENDING messages by Carrier or Homing Pigeon may seem very old-fashioned in this age of electricity and radio waves which make communication with distant places possible, and yet this bird is still used today. During the last war, the United States Army used a Carrier Pigeon service consisting of 150 officers, 3,000 soldiers, and 36,000 well-trained Pigeons. These birds took part in landings in Europe and in bush warfare in the Pacific and in Burma. Some of their number were the first to announce the success of the landing of parachutists in France on June 6, 1944. Some of these Pigeons received medals usually reserved for people.

The history of the Carrier Pigeon goes back to the earliest times, for the Persians, the Greeks, and the Romans used its services. To a layman, the Carrier Pigeon looks no different from the ordinary Pigeon. However, it has longer wings and stronger chest muscles which give the bird a heavier appearance. It is trained to return to its cote after being freed at greater and greater distances from it, sometimes hundreds of miles. Then it is encouraged to return to a movable Pigeon house, which is essential in times of war.

The Homing Pigeon is used most by amateurs, who organize contests to test the sense of direction of their birds.

Birds and Nature

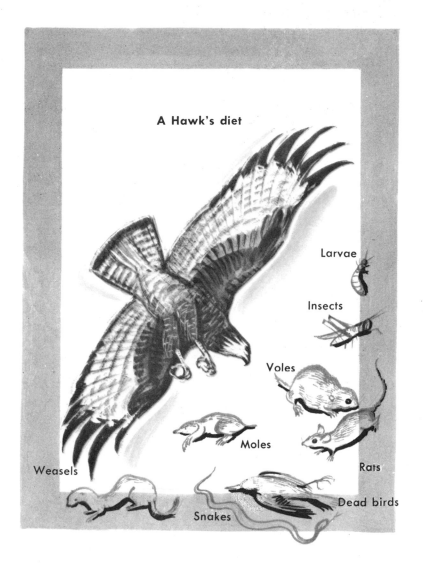

A Hawk's diet

Larvae

Insects

Voles

Moles

Rats

Weasels

Dead birds

Snakes

In tropical Africa, huge swarms of locusts descend upon crops. They are followed by thousands of birds of prey, including Storks and Shrikes, which feed on the locusts, thereby destroying millions of harmful insects.

We have employed chemicals in our fight against insects, using many insecticides to spray fields and orchards. This method is very effective, but it is no substitute for birds. A Woodpecker can extract harmful insects hidden in the bark of trees, and a Warbler or Chaffinch finds insects to eat under leaves. Birds are far more effective in destroying insects than are insecticides, which destroy helpful bees as well as crop-eating insects.

In keeping birds around us we should leave our surroundings as much as possible in their natural state and not be forever raking, pruning and chopping. Insects are attracted to a dead or dying tree, and birds are attracted by insects. Chickadees and Titmice nest in holes in dead branches. Woodpeckers and Owls nest in holes of dead trees. We can also provide cover to attract and keep birds secure. Cover can be of many sorts including thickets, bushes, brush piles, hedges, unkempt corners, briar patches, and piles of logs or debris. Each of these provides birds with a shelter and a place where they can rest and hide from their enemies.

Without birds, the earth would be a wasteland. We could never do without these precious helpers. By ridding us of parasites, birds make themselves useful in one of the best of all ways.

WHEN a scavenger hovers over a farmyard, the first instinct of a farmer is to shoot it. Condemning this bird to death, his next action is probably to take down his gun to kill it.

But the farmer is not necessarily right in deciding to do this, for scavengers do a great amount of good. They are one of nature's cleaning forces and feed upon dead and decaying animal flesh of all sorts. They seldom attack living animals, though they sometimes may set upon those that are dying and are too weak to offer resistance.

Fishing with Cormorants in China

Passenger Pigeon

Extinct Birds

Dodo

AT the beginning of the nineteenth century, the eastern part of the United States was the scene of a unique spectacle. Huge numbers of Passenger Pigeons, migrating to the Gulf of Mexico, traveled in such droves that they darkened the sky. Millions flew over the land. Their passing inspired shooting parties, where each person tried to shoot more Pigeons than his neighbor. There was no need to be a good shot, for one had only to fire into the thick mass of birds to bag several at one shot. An ornithologist of this time estimated that there were over two and a quarter million of these Pigeons in a single flock he saw in Kentucky in 1810.

In the spring, Passenger Pigeons returned in huge flocks to nest in Canada and in the northern part of the United States. Trees bent under the weight of nests, and birds were squeezed together side by side. Again there were great massacres of Pigeons. Trees were cut down and young Pigeons were taken from their nests.

The result of these excesses was a rapid decline of Passenger Pigeons. The big flocks began to disappear after 1850, but the hunting continued. Soon Passenger Pigeons were seldom seen. In 1911 a prize of fifteen hundred dollars was offered to the person finding a nesting pair of these pigeons. The prize was never awarded for every effort was in vain. The last survivor of this species, which a hundred years before had been the most prolific in all America, died in 1914 in the Zoological Gardens at Cincinnati. Man had been responsible for the extinction of the entire species.

When we visit a natural history museum, we look at cases displaying thousands of animals from all over the world. Then we see rooms containing fossils. The bones are all that remain of these animals which disappeared from the earth millions of years ago.

Between these two categories of animals, those which disappeared long ago and those which are still living, are those which are disappearing at the present time. To our shame, most of the animals which no longer exist today but which were living only one or two centuries ago have become extinct because of man.

Some examples are the Moas, huge cousins of the

Ostriches, which lived in New Zealand, and the Madagascan Aepyornis. These birds were about twelve feet high. They disappeared in the fifteenth century without ever being seen alive by a European.

The Dodos and Solitaires were huge Pigeons which inhabited a few islands in the Indian Ocean, especially Reunion Island. They weighed more than forty-four pounds and were much sought after by sailors who were short of food. As these birds could not fly, they were soon exterminated in the eighteenth century, either by men or by their dogs which destroyed the eggs even if they could not catch the birds. We have some rather indistinct paintings of these birds, as well as a few bones, which help to give us some idea of the appearance of the Dodo.

The Hawaiian Islands were once inhabited by splendid birds about the size of a Sparrow but with bright red or yellow plumage. The natives of the islands used the feathers to make royal robes, greatly diminishing the numbers of these tiny birds.

Great Auk

New Zealand Moa

Three birds which disappeared in the last century were the Cuban Macaw, the Amazon Parrots of the Antilles, and the Bourbon Island Hoopoe.

The Great Auks which lived in the frozen Arctic once nested along the shores of Northern Canada, as well as in Greenland and Scandinavia. As they were unable to fly because of their very short wings, sailors found them easy to catch. The men either ate the birds or used them as bait for fishing, so the Great Auks, too, began to disappear. The last survivors were seen in 1844 on a small islet off the coast of Iceland where they used to breed.

The lovely Carolina Parakeet was shot to extinction by 1920. The last Heath Hen died in 1931. Numbers of Eskimo Curlews which once flocked over the prairies in migration were slaughtered to extinction. The last of this species was reported from Texas in April, 1959.

The list of extinct birds is long. It contains as many as fifty species, all of which disappeared during recent times because of man's lack of foresight.

The list is growing longer, for many species have become extremely rare and are in danger of becoming extinct. The American Whooping Crane is now represented by only thirty-two individuals, and it is feared that in spite of rather belated protection it, too, may soon die out.

Anyone interested in birds hopes that there will always be plenty of birds around—for him to enjoy and for his children to enjoy after him. To assure this it is necessary to practice wise conservation.

101

Bird Protection

MANY of our familiar birds are becoming rare. This is the result of unrestricted hunting. Even today people in various countries kill thousands of small birds for food. A little passerine provides man with less than an ounce of meat and yet alive protects acres of crops far more effectively than expensive insecticides do.

Most birds can live only in a particular environment. Some are forest birds, others live in hedgerows and others on marshy land. The main threat to birds today is not the hunter and his gun but the man with the bulldozer. With the growth of cities and industries, the construction of roads and factories, came the destruction of the birds' habitats, in fields and woods and swamps. Wetlands of swamps, marshes, and meadows are threatened by continual drainage and filling. Shores and beaches are menaced by the construction of summer resorts. Habitat is the most important thing to protect if we are to save our birds.

Men of good will have gone to great lengths to protect birds. They have created vast reserves and national parks where it is forbidden to kill any animal or to transform the countryside they inhabit. There are countless areas where birds are protected in the United States. Chief among them are the 173 national parks and monuments, with a surface area of over 21 million acres. There are also the Federal Bird Reservations, founded in 1903, which cover 18 million acres. In addition, there are the many reserves maintained by the Audubon Society. This unique organization has built a network of remarkable reserves and protects some of our finest birds, especially in the southeast where many water birds not so long ago were threatened with extinction.

One example of better living room for birds is a waterfowl sanctuary set up by the government in

A game warden from the National Audubon Society

1934 called the Mattamuskeet National Wildlife Refuge. It has fifty thousand acres of land and shallow, sluggish water in North Carolina. The bird life of Mattamuskeet includes about two hundred different species, mostly water birds and water-loving birds.

Hundreds of reserves have been set up elsewhere in the world. They range from the immense national parks of Africa to tiny refuges where migratory birds can rest during their travels.

These measures are taken by administrative authorities, but we can all help to protect birds. Not only can we support the activities of such groups as the Audubon Society, but we can also play an active part ourselves in safeguarding birds. We can see that nests are safe from animals and discourage egg collectors.

We might put nesting boxes against the trunks of large trees in our gardens. These bird "prefabs" built of wood with a hole about one and a quarter to two and a half inches in diameter are ideal dwellings for Chickadees, Nuthatches, Bluebirds, Wrens, English Sparrows, and Purple Martins. We can also arrange feeding places for birds by placing a plank in a tree about five feet from the ground and sprinkling it with the favorite foods of birds—grain, pumpkin seeds, bread crumbs, and sunflower seeds. Such feeders can be improved upon by the addition of a roof, which enables birds to feed even when it snows. They should also have a few holes in the floor to draw off rain or melting snow. If one feeds birds in winter, it is important to keep it up throughout the entire season, for birds may perish after becoming dependent upon a person for food. Many persons put out food for birds all year round. Summer or winter, birds will always be attracted by a supply of edibles.

We should not forget to put water in an accessible place where birds can come to drink and bathe.

By encouraging birds in these ways we provide a welcoming home for them in our gardens, and we also give ourselves much pleasure in the feeding and looking after of these delightful, feathered creatures.

Nesting box and Flycatcher

A block of suet and seeds hanging from a branch

Cut-away view of a nesting box.

Bird feeder

Bird feeding shelter

103

Did you know that...?

THE WOODCOCK TRANSPORTS ITS YOUNG IN ITS CLAWS

If its nest is disturbed, this careful bird picks up its young with its claws and carries them to a safer place. It will make many trips back and forth until all its chicks are in the new shelter. Ornithologists have also seen Woodcocks carry their young on their backs. Since it would be almost impossible for the mother to place the children on her back herself, ornithologists believe that the young climb over the mother while she is sitting in the nest, much the way chicks and ducklings do. Surprised by a passer-by, the mother probably flies off, and the young clutch her feathers, amazed to find themselves in the air.

THE PAINTED SNIPE HAS SEVERAL HUSBANDS

This member of the Snipe family, who lives in the tropical countries of the Old World, asks her mate to build her a nest of grasses and water plants near the water in the marshlands. She lays eggs and then abandons them, leaving them in the care of the male who takes complete charge of hatching and raising the young. Meanwhile the mother looks for another husband and repeats the whole process, sometimes several times in a year. The female has more attractive feathers than her mate. She is the one who courts, spreading her wings and tail feathers and assuming curious poses. Like all Snipes she makes a strange alarm note when disturbed and flies off in a zigzag fashion. The roles of the male and female are almost completely reversed among these strange birds.

THE TURACOS ARE NOT GUARANTEED "COLORFAST"

These birds of the African forests wear magnificent red purple spots on their wings that contrast with the rest of their green plumage. The coloring is brilliant but if the wings are washed in water, the red spots dissolve and color the water. It was even believed that after a heavy rain these birds' wings were completely discolored. This red pigment, which does not seem to be protected by the thick, horny layers that usually cover feathers, is related to the hemoglobin of human blood, which explains its strong coloring power.

THE AUSTRALIAN SEA GULL BREAKS MOLLUSK SHELLS BY DROPPING THEM FROM THE SKY

Nature did not provide the Sea Gull with a beak strong enough to break hard shells of certain mollusks found on the beaches of Australia. Having found a mollusk in a coral reef, this resourceful bird picks it up, flies with its catch to the rocky cliffs near the shore, and drops it from a considerable height. The shell breaks and the Sea Gull swallows the mollusk in one gulp. Upon finding such a large mound of broken shells which had been built up through the years, naturalists at first believed they had stumbled upon the site of an ancient civilization, in which the people had fed mainly on shellfish.

THE YOUNG WEAVERBIRDS
HAVE PHOSPHORESCENT MOUTHS

The Weaverbird is noted for its intricately woven nests. Some species have nests with one hundred to three hundred compartments. The young Weavers live in closed nests in which there is almost total darkness. Their parents would have much difficulty in finding the beaks of their little ones and filling them with food, if nature had not seen fit to line the edges of their beaks with rims of bright yellow and to place pustules of brilliant color, red or yellow, in their throat cavities. These reflect and shine intensely in the shadows, making effective signaling devices which guide the parents directly to their children's beaks.

BIRDS CAN FLY AT
ASTONISHING HEIGHTS

Geese can fly at a height of 27,000 feet, which poses a physiological problem, because the air is rarefied and the temperatures very low at these altitudes. Many migrants that live in Siberia winter in India, making it necessary for them to cross the Himalayas, the highest mountain chain in the world. Godwits and Ducks have also been observed at 16,000 feet, and Jackdaws at 15,000 feet. But most birds make their trip at much lower altitudes. Little passerines migrate at between one hundred and four hundred feet, some of them even skimming the waves when they cross the sea, in order to be somewhat sheltered from the strong ocean winds.

THE AMERICAN POOR-WILL HIBERNATES
LIKE A MARMOT

The small, gray Poor-Will is a western United States species of the Whip-Poor-Will. While many of its summer companions choose to leave the country during the winter season, the Poor-Will shuns migration, preferring to squeeze itself into a hole in a rock, its head turned toward the dark inside. Then it falls into a deep slumber, during which time all its heart and respiratory movements stop. Its temperature falls from 104º F. to 68º F., exactly as does that of a marmot. It appears to be dead, but actually it is in a state of deep lethargy from which it will emerge as soon as it feels the first warming rays of the spring sun. The Poor-Will is the only bird in the world known to have this habit of hibernation.

THE GRAY PARROT SOWS OIL PALM
TREES IN THE AFRICAN FORESTS

The fruit of these palms form nuts with hard shells and with a savory pulp that is rich in oil. The Gray Parrots crack these nuts with their strong beaks and swallow the pulp inside. Very often they carry a nut off with them to enjoy it in peace, far from other Parrots eager to steal it. But sometimes they drop the nut, losing it in the dense vegetation of the undergrowth. Thus they actually sow the oil palm in the African forests. There is real teamwork between the plant that nourishes the bird and the bird that assures the propagation of the plant, sowing it in new regions.

Did you know that...?

THE AUSTRALIAN BLACK-BREASTED BUZZARD BOMBS THE EGGS IT WANTS TO EAT

The Australian Black-Breasted Buzzard, a bird of prey, is very fond of huge eggs that Emus and Bustards lay in shallow dips in the ground. This bird frightens off its victims by gracefully nose-diving toward the totally exposed nesting bird. Then, as they depart the Buzzard, rather than break the shell with its strong beak, takes a stone or a lump of hard earth in its claws and drops it upon the egg. After that, the banquet is prepared and there is nothing left for the bird to do but to enjoy its catch.

THE ALBATROSS IS LOYAL TO ITS NATIVE LAND

Since time immemorial a large colony of Albatrosses has been established on Midway Island in the middle of the Pacific Ocean. These birds are like giant gulls, weighing around twenty pounds and measuring about four feet from the tip of the tail to the tip of the bill.

Because these birds are dangerous to planes taking off and landing at this busy air base, it was decided to transplant them to places far enough away to prevent their returning. Some were moved to the Philippine Islands, 4,120 miles away; others were taken to the state of Washington, 3,200 miles from Midway. Nevertheless, traveling sometimes as much as 317 miles in one day, they came home. These records show a highly developed sense of orientation in the Albatross.

106

CERTAIN PARROTS LIKE TO EAT SHEEP

The Kea, a Parrot whose green feathers are tinged with red, has a strong and long beak. It lives in the barren zones of the high mountains of New Zealand. In the past, probably because of the lack of vegetation, these usually vegetarian birds were sometimes forced to feed on the dead bodies of mountain sheep. Several among them developed a taste for meat and began to attack live sheep, landing on their backs and tearing off pieces of flesh until the poor beasts died of their wounds. This habit of the Kea soon caused a price to be put on its head in certain regions in which it lived.

In fairness to the Kea, it must be remembered that only some of them developed a taste for meat; the rest were content to go on with their usual diet of fruit and roots.

THE KIWI FOLLOWS ITS NOSE

This wingless bird, found in New Zealand, is not only a living fossil in the modern world, it also is the only bird with a highly developed sense of smell. A night bird, it frequents humid forests where it hunts worms, insects, and larvae crawling on the ground, varying this diet with juicy berries. It would have great difficulties uncovering its prey if nature hadn't provided it with a long beak curved at the end where the nostrils are found. The Kiwi is the only bird that has such a beak. Its sense of smell is extremely acute, enabling it to follow the tracks of its prey or to seek out their hiding places just as a mammal would do.

MOTMOTS PLUCK THEIR TAILS

These South American birds often have long tails, each feather of which ends in a small "racket" at the end of a long rachis. Ornithologists were puzzled for a long time by this absence of barbules along such a great length of each feather and thought that these barbules were probably very fragile and therefore fell off of their own accord. But later it was noticed that the birds plucked them off themselves, by contorting themselves into weird positions and tearing them out with their beaks. No one has yet found the reason for this strange behavior.

ANTS FURNISH BEAUTY PRODUCTS TO BIRDS

One peculiar use of the ant, an insect found in virtually every land area, is to be a beauty product for birds. Starlings, Crows, and other birds take ants in their beaks and rub them against their plumage and even against the skin beneath their feathers, especially along the flanks and at the base of the tail. It is believed that they use the acid and odorous secretions of these insects as an astringent and even as an anti-parasite. It is certainly not used as a perfume, as most birds are supposed to have no sense of smell whatsoever.

BIRDS CAN BECOME DANGEROUS FIREBRANDS

Birds have been seen to dive on burning cigarette butts that passers-by have carelessly dropped in the street, and carry them in their beaks to their nests. The straw and dry twigs catch fire very easily, and a burning nest is enough to start a fire in a building or a forest fire. In the course of the "Great Fire" that destroyed London in 1666 some Jackdaws were seen carrying about torches of burning pieces of straw and thus contributing to the spread of the fire.

THE OYSTER CATCHER WISHES IT HAD LARGER EGGS

Experiments have been made proving that if a model egg, similar in shape and color to the Oyster Catcher's egg but three times as big, is offered to this bird, it will quickly adopt it in preference to its own. Abandoning its own smaller eggs, it will devote its attention to the large artificial one, making great efforts to sit on it and cover it and showing amazement that this artificial egg resists being hatched.

BIRDS NEVER HAVE CRAMPS IN THEIR FEET

Because of their structure, birds' feet are free from cramps. The muscles and tendons of perching birds are so made that when the bird lands, the claws close automatically around the branch and assure a strong hold. In this way birds are able to perch indefinitely without contracting their muscles, and they are also able to go to sleep without falling from their perch.

107

Birds in History

WHEN Christopher Columbus sailed in 1492 to find a westward route to the Indies, he made careful notes in his logbook of the names and numbers of birds he saw on the way. When after a time the sea became quite deserted for days on end, the crew lost all hope of finding land in the west and began to mutiny. Then suddenly a few Gulls appeared, followed by some land birds which came to perch on the ships. The sailors calmed down and their spirits rose. "Land is near," they realized and soon Columbus sighted what he thought was India.

Without the hope these birds inspired, the sailors would not have had the patience to wait for the journey's end. They might have murdered Columbus and tried to return to Spain and the expedition would have been a failure.

There are many other historical incidents in which birds played an important part. When the colonists penetrated the western part of the United States, a group of pioneers settled around Great Salt Lake. In spite of difficult conditions they managed to cultivate the land and grow flourishing crops. When swarms of locusts descended on the fields to eat their crops, the settlers panicked, fearing they would lose everything. But Gulls followed the throng of locusts and fed upon the pests, saving the pioneers' crops. To commemorate this occasion a monument was erected to the glory of the Gulls.

Legend has many tales about birds. The people of ancient Egypt worshiped a bird-god, Horus. This god had the head of a Falcon and the body of a man. In the struggles after the Crusades, the Saracens asked for and got Greenland gyrfalcons as ransom for captured Christian nobles. The ancient sport of falconry was popular with kings and nobles who trained Hawks to hunt other birds and small animals. The Bald Eagle is our national emblem, the Turkey is the symbol of Thanksgiving Day, and the Baltimore Oriole and the Cardinal have lent their names to famous baseball teams. History is full of references to birds, which show the pleasures, profits and marvels these feathered creatures bring to us. It has always been to man's advantage to preserve and protect the bird population of the world.

Pelican

Mallard

Reed Bunting

European Bee-Eater

Purple Heron

Moor Hens

109